Diabetic AirFryer Cookbook

Revolutionize Your Diabetic Diet with Flavorful, Healthy Air Fryer Recipes for Every Meal. Including 30 Days No Stress Meal Plan

Juno Lee-Green & Grace Garner

© **Copyright 2024 - All rights reserved.**

The content contained within this book may not be reproduced, duplicated or transmitted without direct written permission from the author or the publisher.
Under no circumstances will any blame or legal responsibility be held against the publisher, or author, for any damages, reparation, or monetary loss due to the information contained within this book. Either directly or indirectly.
Legal Notice:
This book is copyright protected. This book is only for personal use. You cannot amend, distribute, sell, use, quote or paraphrase any part, or the content within this book, without the consent of the author or publisher.
Disclaimer Notice:
Please note the information contained within this document is for educational and entertainment purposes only. All effort has been executed to present accurate, up to date, and reliable, complete information. No warranties of any kind are declared or implied. Readers acknowledge that the author is not engaging in the rendering of legal, financial, medical or professional advice. The content within this book has been derived from various sources.

By reading this document, the reader agrees that under no circumstances is the author responsible for any losses, direct or indirect, which are incurred as a result of the use of information contained within this document, including, but not limited to, — errors, omissions, or inaccuracies.

ISBN 979-8-39-479835-1

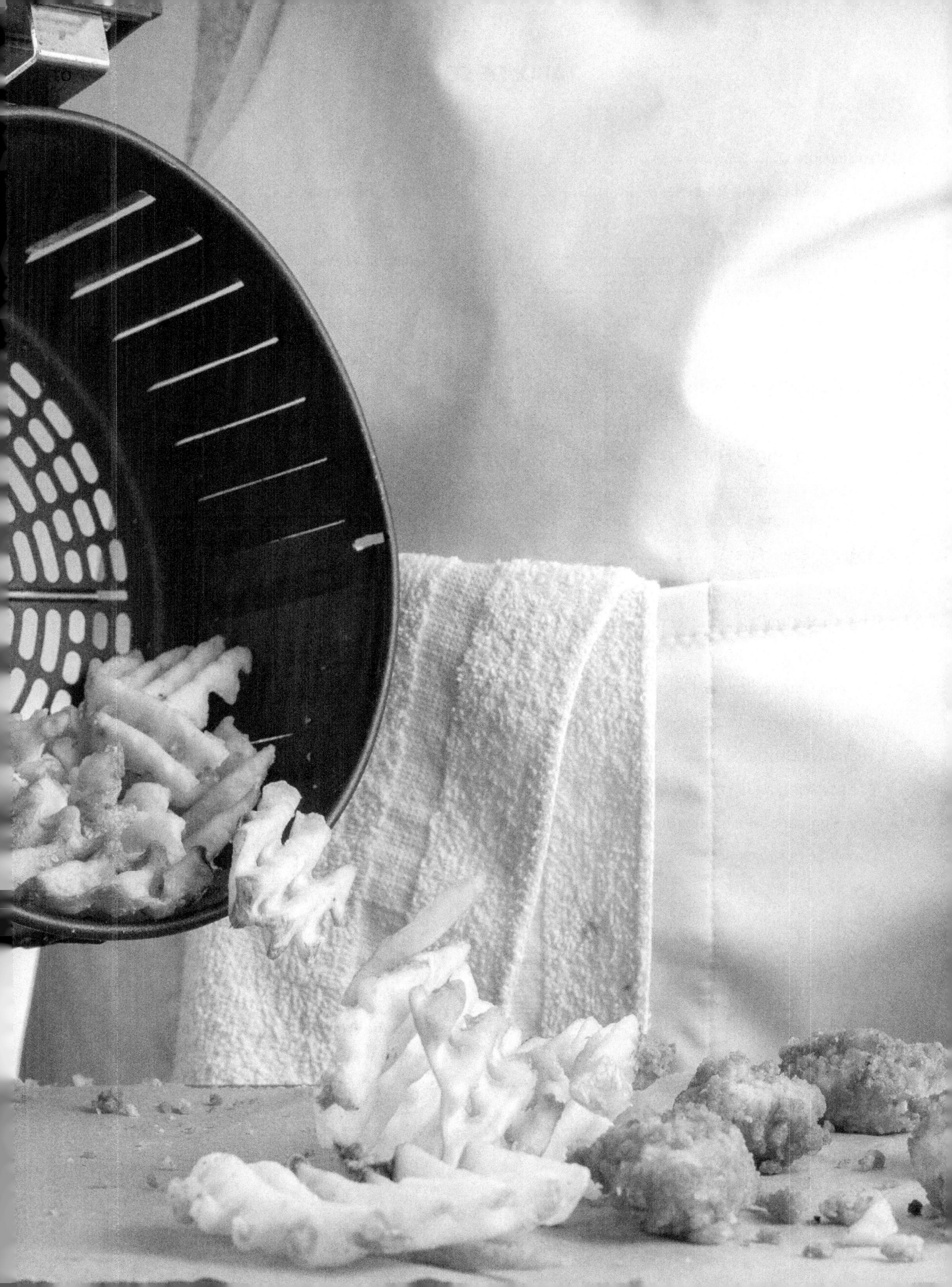

TABLE OF CONTENT

Introduction	7

Chapter 1: Managing Diabetes 8
- Diet and Lifestyle Management 8
- Range of GI Values 9
- Food To Eat 11
- Food To Avoid 11
- Sugar-Free Sweeteners 11

Chapter 02: Why Air Fryers? 13
- How Does an Air Fryer Work? 13
- How To Use an Air Fryer? 13
- Cleaning an Air Fryer 14
- Essential Kitchen Tools 14

Chapter 3: Breakfast 16
- Pumpkin Bread 16
- English Muffin 16
- Apple Cobbler 17
- Banana Churro Oatmeal 17
- Crunchy Breakfast Casserole 18
- Thai Style Omelet 18
- Cheesy Asparagus Frittata 18
- Egg, Bean and Mushroom Burrito 19
- Omelet Cups with Bell Pepper and Onion 19
- Egg and Ham Casserole 20
- Egg Prosciutto 20
- Egg Bites 20
- Scotch Eggs 21
- Broccoli Frittata 21
- Egg Quiche 22
- Low-Carb Granola 22
- Low Carb Flat-Bread 23
- Cauliflower Hash Brown 23
- Egg Zucchini Frittata 24
- Kuku Eggs 24

Chapter 4: Snacks 25
- Chicken Samosa 25
- Zucchini Fries 25
- Cheese Puffs 26
- Avocado Fries 26
- Pickle Fries 27
- Kale Chips 27
- Onion Rings 27
- Plantains Chips 28
- Jalapeno Poppers 28
- Pepperoni Chips 28
- Spicy Peanuts 29
- Chicken Nuggets 29
- Mozzarella Sticks 30
- Carrot Fries 30
- Bacon Wrapped Avocado Wedge 31
- Bacon Wrapped Jalapeno Peppers 31
- Eggplant Fries 32
- Cassava Fries 32
- Cauliflower Croquettes 33
- Zucchini Fritters 33
- Bacon Wrapped Zucchini Fries 34
- Cassava Croquettes 34

Chapter 5: Poultry 35
- Chicken Kiev 35
- Chicken Broccoli 35
- Chicken Teriyaki 36
- Stuffed Chicken Breast 36
- Dragon Chicken 37
- Chicken Meatloaf 37
- Chicken Tenders 38

Spinach Stuffed Chicken 38
Bacon Wrapped Chicken 39
Chicken Breast Asparagus Rolls 39
Chicken Drumsticks 39
Tandoori Chicken 40
Chicken Mushroom Skewers 41
Chicken Satay 41
Chicken Fajita 42
Chicken Cordon Blue 42
Stuffed Turkey Rolls 43
Stuffed Whole Chicken 43
Pesto Chicken 44
Chicken Parmesan 44
Chicken Casserole 44
Herbed Turkey Breast 45
Duck Breast Fillet 45

Chapter 6: Seafood 46
Teriyaki Shrimp 46
Spinach Stuffed Salmon 46
Parmesan Calamari 47
Crusted Cod 47
Crusted Scallops 47
Fish Schnitzel 48
Shrimp Fajita 48
Fish Tacos 49
Bacon Wrapped Shrimp 49
Bacon Wrapped Scallop 50
Shrimp Kung Pao 50
Fish Sticks 50
Fried Mahi-Mahi 51
Maple Glazed Tuna Steaks 51
Crispy Oysters 52
Crusted Haddock 52
Crab Rangoon 53

Crab Stuffed Mushrooms 53
Tuna Patties 54
Blackened Salmon 54

Chapter 7: Pork, Beef and Lamb 55
Meatball Subs 55
Garlicky Buttery Steak Bites 55
Steak Tips with Roasted Potatoes 56
Bacon Wrapped Filet Mignon 56
Mongolian Beef 56
Pepperoni Pizza 57
Cheese Stuffed Kebabs 57
Stuffed Bell Pepper 58
Sweet Sticky Pork Chops 58
Pork Schnitzel 59
Beef Hamburgers 59
Mushroom Stuffed Pork 60
Bacon Wrapped Pork Tenderloin 61
Roasted Pork Tenderloin 61
Pork Skewers 61
Pork Mushroom Skewer 62
Chimichurri Lamb Chop 62
Beef Fajita 63
Lamb Kebab 63
Beef Meatloaf 64
Cajun Pork Chops 64

Chapter 8: Vegetarian Recipes 65
Cauliflower Steak 65
Broccoli Parmesan 65
Stuffed Butternut Squash 66
Fried Okra 66
Crusted Mushroom 67
Mushroom Skewers 67
Eggplant Parmesan 68
Ratatouille 68

Tofu Satay 69
Tofu Pineapple Skewer............................. 69
Crispy Broccoli Salad 70
Oyster Mushroom 70
Tofu Popcorn 70
Spicy Black Beans 71
Spaghetti Squash...................................... 71
Kale Potato Nuggets 71
Buffalo Tofu... 72
Buffalo Cauliflower.................................... 72
Bang Bang Cauliflower 73
Parmesan Brussel Sprouts....................... 73
Hush Puppies 74
BBQ Lentil Meatballs................................ 74
Crispy Soy Curls 75
Blooming Onion 75

Chapter 9: Dessert 76
Walnut Brownie 76
Carrot Cake with Cream Cheese Frosting........ 76
Zebra Cake... 77
Cream Cheese Stuffed Lava Cake 78
Chocolate Donut 78
Coffee Cake 79
Shortbread Cookies.................................. 79
Butter Pecan Cake 80
Churros... 81
Low-Carbs Cupcakes................................ 81
Chocolate Chip Cookies............................ 82
Blueberry Cobbler 82
Carrot Cupcakes....................................... 83
Red velvet Cake 83
Cherry Pie... 84
Citrus Cake 84
Chocolate Hazelnut Muffins...................... 85

Cookie Cake 85
Pumpkin Pie Twists 86
Cinnamon Bread Twits............................. 86
30 Days Meal-Plan....................................87
30 Days Shopping 94
Measurement Conversion Table 96
Weight conversion tables 96
Liquid Conversion Table........................... 96
Conclusion...97

Introduction

Navigating the challenges of living with diabetes can be daunting, but with the right approach to lifestyle and diet, it's possible to maintain a healthy, active, and fulfilling life. With a concerning 1 in every 10 adults in the US suffering from diabetes, it's crucial for us to proactively plan our lifestyles and diets to address the risk factors associated with diabetes and other chronic illnesses. The diabetic-friendly diet is specifically designed to advocate for portion control and provide a comprehensive list of low-glycemic foods that won't cause an immediate spike in blood sugar levels. By steering clear of high-sugar, high-carb, and high-glycemic foods, this diet has proven effective in managing type 2 diabetes while simultaneously promoting a healthy, active, and fit lifestyle for those who follow it

Obesity is a significant contributing factor that can lead to the development of diabetes or exacerbate complications if you are already diagnosed with the condition. Health experts unanimously recommend that by successfully reducing caloric intake, cutting back on high-fat foods, and practicing portion control, it is possible to minimize the harmful impact of this disease. This is where the revolutionary air fryer comes into play! Air fryers have transformed the way we enjoy our favorite indulgences by allowing us to savor finger-licking, crispy fried foods with a remarkable 70 percent less oil content compared to traditional deep-frying methods.

When someone dear and close to me was diagnosed with diabetes, investing in an air fryer became an essential step in helping them manage their condition. Since then, I have been using it to create a diverse range of meals, from satisfying breakfast options to mouthwatering entrees, scrumptious snacks, delightful appetizers, and even low-carb desserts tailored to diabetics. The 150 diabetic-friendly recipes I am about to share in the cookbook are my personal favorites, each thoroughly tested in my home kitchen. From crispy chicken nuggets and savory meatballs to zesty fish tacos and veggie-packed dishes, these recipes are perfect for busy weeknights or weekend gatherings I encourage you to give them a try and experience the delicious benefits for yourself. But first, let's take a moment to explore the fundamentals of a diabetic diet and how it relates to the incredible capabilities of air fryers in our quest for healthier living.

And don't forget, as a special thank you for joining me on this journey, I've included three exclusive bonuses—make sure to check out page 98 to discover how to enhance your culinary adventure!

Chapter 1: Managing Diabetes

Diet and Lifestyle Management

Managing type 2 diabetes requires a multifaceted approach that includes diet and lifestyle modifications in addition to medication when necessary. Here are some tips for managing type 2 diabetes through diet and lifestyle changes:

Follow a balanced and healthy diet: A balanced diet that includes a variety of whole foods such as low glycemic fruits, non-starchy vegetables, whole grains, proteins (lean), and healthy fats can help to control blood sugar levels. Limiting processed and high-sugar foods are also important.

Uphold a healthy weight: Carrying excess body weight is a significant player in the risk of developing type 2 diabetes. Shedding even a minor portion of weight can result in an enhancement in the management of blood sugar levels.

Engage in physical activity: Consistent physical activity can foster greater insulin sensitivity and better control of blood sugar. Strive to attain no less than 30 minutes of exercise with moderate intensity on most days of the week.

Manage stress: Chronic stress can increase blood sugar levels, so it's important to find ways to manage stress, such as practicing mindfulness, deep breathing, or engaging in relaxing activities.

Get enough sleep: Poor sleep can affect blood sugar control, so aim for at least 7-8 hours of sleep per night.

Monitor blood sugar levels: Regular monitoring of blood sugar levels can help to identify patterns and adjust diet and medication as needed.

Seek support: Managing type 2 diabetes can be overwhelming, so it's important to seek support from family, friends, healthcare providers, or support groups.

Remember, managing type 2 diabetes is a lifelong journey, and making little changes to your lifestyle and diet can have a big impact on your health and well-being. Working closely with a healthcare provider to develop a personalized plan for managing diabetes is key to success.

What Is a Diabetic Friendly Diet?

A diabetic-friendly diet is an eating plan designed to help manage blood sugar levels in people with diabetes. It involves making healthy food choices that are low in added sugars and refined carbohydrates while still providing adequate nutrients to support overall health. One key aspect of a diabetic-friendly diet is managing carbohydrate intake. Carbohydrates are important nutrients that the body uses for energy, but too many carbohydrates, especially refined carbohydrates, can cause blood sugar levels to spike. A diabetic-friendly diet typically involves monitoring portion sizes and choosing foods that have a low glycemic index (GI). Foods with a low GI release glucose into the bloodstream slowly, which can help to prevent spikes in blood sugar levels. In addition to managing carbohydrates, a diabetic-friendly diet typically emphasizes whole foods such as fruits, vegetables, whole grains, lean proteins, and healthy fats. These food items are high in nutrients and fiber, which can help to enhance overall health and reduce the risk of other health complications associated with diabetes, such as heart disease.

It's also important to limit or avoid processed and high-sugar foods, as well as high-fat foods that can contribute to weight gain. Sugary beverages, such as soda and juice, should also be limited or avoided. Besides making healthy food choices, a diabetic-friendly diet also involves managing portion sizes and eating small, frequent meals throughout the day. This can help to manage blood sugar levels and prevent spikes and crashes.

Working closely with a registered dietitian or healthcare provider is key to developing a personalized meal plan that fits individual needs and preferences. A healthcare provider may also recommend regular blood sugar monitoring to help identify patterns and adjust the diet as needed.

What Is Glycemic Index?

The concept of the glycemic index has gained interest among both nutrition experts and health enthusiasts. At the heart of the glycemic index lies the idea of how rapidly carbohydrates in food elevate blood sugar levels. The rate at which glucose is released into the bloodstream after consumption is what determines the glycemic index of a food. Foods with a high glycemic index cause a rapid and significant spike in blood sugar levels, while foods with a low glycemic index release glucose more slowly and steadily. A glycemic index is a valuable tool for understanding how different foods affect our bodies and can be used to make decisions about what we eat. Whether you're looking to manage diabetes, lose weight, or simply improve your overall health, understanding the glycemic index is essential for making informed choices about your diet.

Why Should We Eat Low GI Food?

Eating low-glycemic food helps regulate blood sugar levels. High GI foods, such as processed and refined carbohydrates, are quickly digested and absorbed, causing a rapid increase in blood sugar levels. This can be particularly problematic for people with diabetes, as their bodies may not produce enough insulin or may be resistant to insulin, which is needed to regulate blood sugar levels.

Eating low-GI foods, on the other hand, can help to manage blood sugar levels and prevent spikes and crashes. Low GI foods are digested and absorbed slowly, leading to a slower and more gradual increase in blood sugar levels. This can help to prevent hyperglycemia (high blood sugar) and reduce the need for insulin or other blood sugar-lowering medications.

In addition, eating low-GI foods can also provide other health benefits, such as improved satiety and reduced risk of heart disease. Low GI foods tend to be rich in fiber, which can help to achieve feelings of fullness and prevent overeating. They also tend to be nutrient-dense, providing a wide variety of vitamins, minerals, and antioxidants that can help to support overall health.

How Is the Glycemic Index Calculated?

GI, or the Glycemic Index of food, is a measure of how quickly the carbs in the food are broken down and absorbed into the bloodstream, which affects blood sugar levels. Here are the general steps to calculate the glycemic index of a food:

- Choose a food: Select the food that you want to calculate the GI for.
- Test subjects: You will need at least 10 healthy subjects for the testing.
- Testing: The testing will involve measuring the blood glucose levels of the subjects at specific time intervals after they consume a serving of the test food. This is done by giving them a fixed amount of the test food and measuring their blood glucose levels at regular intervals (usually every 15-30 minutes) for several hours after they eat.
- Control: A control food with a known GI is also included to ensure that the testing conditions are consistent.
- Calculate: The GI is calculated by dividing the area under the blood glucose curve for the test food by the area under the blood glucose curve for the control food and then multiplying by 100. The resulting number is the GI of the test food.

Range of GI Values

Once the GI values of the food items are calculated they are then categorized according to the following standards:

High GI foods: 70 or above. Examples include white bread, rice cakes, instant oatmeal, corn flakes, watermelon, and baked potatoes. Food belonging to category must either be avoided or be taken in a very small amount on a diabetic diet.

Medium GI foods: 56 to 69. Examples include whole wheat bread, brown rice, sweet potato, pineapple, and honey. These food items can be taken in moderation.

Low GI foods: 55 or below. Examples include most vegetables, legumes, fruits (except watermelon and pineapple), nuts, and whole grain foods like barley, quinoa, and steel-cut oats. The low GI foods are most suitable for a low-carb diet.

GI Values for Fruits

Here are some glycemic indices for commonly consumed fruits, arranged in descending order:

- Watermelon: 72
- Pineapple: 66
- Mango: 51
- Papaya: 56
- Banana: 51
- Grapes: 46
- Orange: 45
- Apple: 39
- Pear: 38
- Peach: 28
- Plum: 24
- Cherries: 22
- Grapefruit: 25
- Strawberries: 40
- Blueberries: 53

GI Values of Vegetables

Here are some glycemic indices for commonly consumed vegetables, arranged in descending order:

- Carrots: 47
- Pumpkin: 75
- Parsnips: 97
- Sweet potato: 70
- Potato (boiled): 78
- Corn: 60
- Beets: 64
- Peas: 54
- Green peas: 51
- Broccoli: 10
- Cauliflower: 15
- Cabbage: 10
- Eggplant: 15
- Bell peppers: 15
- Tomatoes: 15

GI Values of Grains

Here are some glycemic indices for commonly consumed grains and grain products, arranged in descending order:

- White bread: 75
- Whole wheat bread: 74
- Brown rice: 68
- White rice: 73
- Oatmeal: 55
- Instant oatmeal: 79
- Barley: 25-36
- Bulgur: 46
- Quinoa: 53
- Corn tortilla: 46
- White pasta: 45
- Brown pasta: 65
- Couscous: 65
- Buckwheat: 54
- Rye bread: 64

GI Values of Legumes

Here are some glycemic indices for commonly consumed legumes, arranged in descending order:

- Baked beans: 48
- Chickpeas: 28
- Black beans: 30
- Kidney beans: 24
- Lentils: 32
- Split peas: 32
- Hummus: 6-16
- Soybeans: 18
- Peanuts: 13

GI Values of Sweeteners

Here are some glycemic indices for commonly used sweeteners, arranged in descending order:

- Glucose: 100
- Maltodextrin: 85
- High fructose corn syrup: 62
- Honey: 58
- Sucrose (table sugar): 65
- Maple syrup: 54
- Agave nectar: 15-30

- Stevia: 0
- Erythritol: 0
- Xylitol: 13

GI Values of Dairy Products

Most dairy products have a low GI because they contain minimal carbohydrates and are rich in protein and fat. Here are some examples:

- Whole milk: 41
- Skim milk: 32
- Yogurt (plain, low-fat): 14-19
- Cottage cheese: 10

Food To Eat

Non-starchy vegetables: broccoli, spinach, kale, carrots, green beans, bell peppers, zucchini, cauliflower, and more.

- **Fruits:** berries, apples, pears, oranges, grapefruit, kiwi, and more. It's imperative to be mindful of portion sizes and choose whole fruits instead of fruit juice.
- **Whole grains**: brown rice, quinoa, barley, whole wheat bread, and whole grain pasta.
- **Lean protein sources**: chicken, turkey, fish, tofu, legumes (beans, lentils, chickpeas), and low-fat dairy products.
- **Healthy fats**: avocado, nuts, seeds, olive oil, and fatty fish such as salmon.
- **Low-fat dairy**: milk, yogurt, and cheese.
- **Water and other non-sweetened beverages**: water, unsweetened tea, and coffee.

Food To Avoid

Here is a list of foods that you should avoid or limit as part of a healthy and balanced diet:

- **Sugar-sweetened beverages**: regular soda, fruit punch, sweetened tea, and sports drinks.
- **Processed and refined carbohydrates**: white bread, white rice, pasta, and baked goods made with white flour.
- **Trans and saturated fats:** fried foods, fast food, high-fat dairy products, and fatty meats.
- **High-sodium foods**: canned soups, processed meats, and salty snacks.
- **Sweet treats**: candy, cookies, cakes, and other sweets that are high in added sugars.
- **Alcohol:** drinking alcohol can cause fluctuations in blood sugar levels and should be consumed in moderation or avoided altogether.

Sugar-Free Sweeteners

When it comes to diabetic diet, natural sugars like cane sugar, brown sugar, processed sugar, honey, molasses, and sugar syrup are simply not an option as they spike the blood sugar levels. These high-carb sweeteners must be avoided to keep meals low-carb. Fortunately, there are now several low carb sweeteners which are great at adding the sugar like taste without raising the carb content. These artificial sweeteners come in different intensities and textures, which should be considered when using them. Here is a list of the recommended low-carb sweeteners, let me tell how to use them:

Swerve:

Swerve sweetener is a popular sugar substitute that is commonly used in low-carb diets. The reason why I recommend Swerve in all my low-carb recipes is that it is a natural sweetener prepared from a combination of erythritol, oligosaccharides, and natural flavors. Since it contains only some percentage of erythritol it is not harmful for digestive system and it is easy to digest. Whereas high amount of erythritol intake might cause indigestion in some individuals. Plus you can replace sugar with its equal amount, the sugar-Swerve measurement conversion is super easy.

Swerve sweetener has zero calories, zero net carbs, and is low glycemic, making it a great alternative to sugar for people who want to reduce their sugar intake or maintain a low-carb diet. It comes in both granular and powdered form, and can be used in baking, cooking, and as a sweetener for beverages. It has a sweetness level similar to sugar and does not have a bitter aftertaste like some other sugar substitutes. Additionally, Swerve does not raise blood sugar levels, making it a safe option for people with diabetes or those who are following a low-carb diet.

Stevia:

It is a natural sweetener derived from the leaves of the Stevia Rebaudiana plant, which is native to South America. The sweet taste of Stevia comes from two compounds in the plant's leaves, called Stevioside and Rebaudioside A. Stevia is used as a sugar substitute and is known for its intense sweetness, which is approximately 200-350 times sweeter than sugar. Since stevia is too sweet, I would recommend you to use it as a slight mistake in measurement can throw the entire balance of a recipe of the track. Use it only when you are sure of the measurements.

Erythritol:

Erythritol is a natural sweetener that belongs to the family of sugar alcohols. It is found naturally in some fruits and fermented foods but is mostly commercially produced by fermenting glucose with yeast or other microorganisms. Erythritol has a sweetness level that is about 70% as sweet as sugar but has a negligible effect on blood sugar and insulin levels, making it a popular sugar substitute for people who are watching their sugar intake or following a low-carb, ketogenic or diabetic diet. This sweetener must be taken in moderation to keep your digestive system running.

Monk fruit extract:

It is a natural sweetener derived from the monk fruit. It has no carbohydrates and does not raise blood sugar levels.

Measurement Conversion Table

Sugar	1 tsp	1 Tbsp	1/4 cup	1/3 cup	1/2 cup	1 cup
Swerve	1 tsp	1 Tbsp	1/4 cup	1/3 cup	1/2 cup	1 cup
Erythritol	1 1/4 tsp	1 Tbsp + 1 tsp	1/3 cup	1/3 cup + 2 Tbsp	2/3 cup	1 1/3 cup
Liquid Stevia	3/8 tsp	3/8 tsp	1 1/2 tsp	2 tsp	3 tsp	2 tbsp
Monk fruit	1 tsp	1 Tbsp	1/4 cup	1/3 cup	1/2 cup	1 cup
Stevia Extract	-	-	3/16 tsp	1/4 tsp	3/8 tsp	3/4 tsp

Chapter 02: Why Air Fryers?

The oil-free cooking technology makes air fryers a must-have for everyone, especially those who want to live healthily and keep their weight in check and their blood cholesterol levels controlled. Air fryers use hot air, which circulates around the food, to create a crispy texture similar to fried food without the need for deep frying in oil. This can be particularly beneficial for diabetics who may need to limit their intake of added fats and oils to manage their blood sugar levels and overall health.

In addition, air frying can be a convenient and time-saving way to prepare healthy meals at home. Many air fryer recipes are simple and quick to prepare and can be customized to fit individual dietary needs and preferences. They can be used to cook a wide variety of foods, like vegetables, meats, and even desserts, making them a versatile tool for all of us who are looking to incorporate healthy and flavorful meals into our diets.

How Does an Air Fryer Work?

Imagine enjoying the taste and texture of your favorite fried meal without the guilt of consuming excess oil and fat. That's where the air fryer comes in! This modern kitchen appliance uses hot air circulation to cook food, providing a crispy and delicious result that rivals traditional deep-frying methods. The best part? You can achieve that desirable crunch with just a fraction of the oil needed for deep frying, making it a healthier and more diabetes-friendly option.

The science behind the air fryer is fascinating. By using a combination of a heating element and a powerful fan, hot air is circulated rapidly around the food, cooking it to perfection in no time. It's incredibly easy to use too! Simply place your food in the basket, adjust the temperature and cooking time, and let the air fryer work its magic. Plus, with its compact size and sleek design, it won't take up too much space on your countertop.

When it comes to managing diabetes, using an air fryer can be a game-changer. It allows you to enjoy your favorite foods without compromising your health. Whether it's crispy chicken wings, roasted vegetables, or even sweet potato fries, the air fryer can help you create delicious and healthy meals that are perfect for a diabetic-friendly diet.

How To Use an Air Fryer?

Air fryers have certainly taken the culinary world by storm with their convenience and ease of use. With the ability to cook a wide range of foods, from crispy fries to succulent chicken, air fryers have quickly become a staple in many households. Gone are the days of deep-frying and using copious amounts of oil; air fryers require little to no oil, making them a healthier option. Furthermore, they are easy to clean and maintain, saving time in the kitchen. It doesn't matter if you are a novice cook or a seasoned one; an air fryer can make mealtime effortless and enjoyable. So why not join the bandwagon and experience the convenience and deliciousness of air fryers? Here is how you can use them:

Step 1: Preheat the air fryer

Before using the air fryer, it's important to preheat it for a few minutes to ensure that the cooking basket is heated evenly. Simply set the desired temperature and let the air fryer preheat for 2-3 minutes.

Step 2: Prepare the food

While your air fryer is preheating, you can prepare the food that you want to cook. Cut the food into the desired size and shape, and season it with herbs, spices, or marinades if desired.

Step 3: Arrange the food in the cooking basket

Open the air fryer and place the food in the cooking basket, ensuring that it's arranged in a single layer for even cooking. If you're cooking multiple items, make sure that there is enough space between them to allow for air circulation.

Step 4: Set the cooking time and temperature

Select the desired cooking temperature and time based on the type of food you're cooking. Most air fryers have a digital display that allows you to adjust the settings easily. Refer to the recipe or cooking instructions for guidance on the appropriate time and temperature settings.

Step 5: Start the cooking process

Once you've set the time and temperature, close the air fryer and start the cooking process. The hot air will begin to circulate around the food, cooking it evenly and creating a crispy exterior.

Step 6: Check the food periodically

It's important to check the food periodically during the cooking process to ensure that it's cooking evenly and not burning. Open the air fryer and use tongs or a spatula to flip or shake the food if necessary.

Step 7: Remove the food and serve

Once the cooking time is up, open the air fryer and carefully remove the cooking basket. Use tongs or a spatula to transfer the food to a serving plate.

Cleaning an Air Fryer

Cleaning an air fryer is an important step in maintaining its performance and prolonging its lifespan. Here are the steps to clean an air fryer:

Step 1: Unplug the air fryer

Before cleaning the air fryer, make sure that it's unplugged and has completely cooled down. This will prevent any accidents or injuries.

Step 2: Remove the cooking basket and tray

Carefully remove the cooking basket and tray from the air fryer. Some models may have removable parts that are dishwasher safe, so check the instructions to see if this is an option.

Step 3: Soak the parts in warm, soapy water

Fill a sink or bowl with some warm water and add 2-3 drops of dish soap. Place the cooking basket and tray in the water and let them soak for about 10-15 minutes.

Step 4: Scrub the parts with a non-abrasive sponge or brush

Using a non-abrasive sponge or brush, scrub the cooking basket and tray to remove any leftover food particles or grease. Pay extra attention to any hard-to-reach areas, such as corners or crevices.

Step 5: Rinse and dry the parts

Rinse the cooking basket and tray with clean water to remove any soap residue. Shake off any excess water and dry them thoroughly with a clean towel or allow its parts to air dry completely before placing them back in the air fryer.

Step 6: Clean the exterior

Using a damp cloth, wipe down the exterior of the air fryer to remove any dirt, grime, or grease. Avoid using harsh and abrasive cleaners or steel wool, as these can damage the surface of the air fryer.

Step 7: Reassemble the air fryer

Once all the parts are clean and dry, reassemble the air fryer and store it in a safe place until you're ready to use it again.

Essential Kitchen Tools

Essential kitchen tools play a crucial role in every culinary adventure, whether it's a speedy breakfast or a grand feast, they are the unsung heroes that ensure success. While air fryers are pretty convenient to use kitchen appliance, you are still going to use some kitchen supplies to cook your routine meals up to perfection. So, here is what you are going to need:

Cooking spray:

Cooking spray is an essential tool when air frying as it helps prevent food from sticking to the air fryer basket. It creates a non-stick surface that is particularly useful when cooking delicate items such as fish or tofu. In addition to preventing sticking, cooking spray helps with browning and can add flavor to air-fried food when using a flavored cooking spray. Furthermore, it reduces cleaning time since food is less likely to stick to the basket. When using cooking spray, it's important to use it sparingly as too much can cause food to become greasy. It's also crucial to choose a cooking spray that is safe for use with high temperatures as some may not be suitable for use in an air fryer.

Tongs:

They allow you to safely handle food without having to touch it with your hands. This is especially important when cooking items that are hot or difficult to handle, such as chicken wings or fish. Tongs also give you more control over the food, making it easier to flip or turn items during the cooking process.

Oven mitts or heat-resistant gloves:

These are used to protect your hands when removing the air fryer basket from the machine, which can get hot.

Meat thermometer:

This is used to ensure that the internal temperature of the food is cooked to the desired level of doneness.

Parchment paper:

This can be used to line the air fryer basket to prevent food from sticking and make cleanup easier.

Baking dish:

When using an air fryer, it's important to use bakeware that is safe and compatible with the machine. Some types of baking dishes that are suitable for use in air fryers include:

- Oven-safe glass bakeware - such as Pyrex or Anchor Hocking, are generally safe to use in an air fryer. However, it's important to make sure that the dish is not too large to fit inside the air fryer basket.
- Ceramic bakeware - such as stoneware or porcelain, can also be used in an air fryer as long as they are oven-safe.
- Silicone baking dishes - are a great choice for air fryers, as they are flexible and easy to clean.
- Metal baking dishes - such as stainless steel or aluminum, are also suitable for use in air fryers. However, it's important to make sure that the dish is not too large to fit

inside the air fryer basket, and that it does not have any non-stick coating, as this can scratch the air fryer basket.

When choosing a baking dish for use in an air fryer, it's important to check the manufacturer's instructions to ensure that the bakeware is safe for use in an air fryer.

Food Prep Tools:

Food prep tools are a set of kitchen utensils and tools that are essential for preparing ingredients before cooking. These tools help to make food preparation easier and more efficient. Some common food prep tools include:

- Knives - used for cutting, chopping, slicing, and dicing various ingredients.
- Cutting boards - used to protect countertops while cutting and chopping ingredients.
- Mixing bowls - used for combining ingredients together for recipes.
- Measuring cups and spoons - used to measure out ingredients accurately.
- Graters - used for grating cheese, vegetables, and fruits.
- Vegetable peelers - used to remove the skin from fruits and vegetables.
- Colanders - used for draining pasta and washing vegetables.
- Kitchen scissors - used for cutting meat, vegetables, and herbs.
- Can opener - used for opening canned ingredients.
- Spatulas - used for flipping and turning food while cooking.
- Whisks - used for blending and mixing ingredients together.
- Garlic press - used for mincing garlic cloves.

Having these food prep tools on hand can make cooking much easier and more enjoyable, as they help to streamline the process of preparing ingredients and save time.

Chapter 3: Breakfast

Pumpkin Bread

Prep time: 20 minutes. | **Cook time:** 35 minutes. | **Serves:** 6

Ingredients:

- 1 cup almond flour
- ¼ cup coconut flour
- ½ cup pumpkin puree
- ¼ cup Swerve
- 2 eggs
- 1 teaspoon baking powder
- 1 teaspoon pumpkin pie spice
- ¼ teaspoon salt
- ¼ cup unsweetened almond milk
- 1 teaspoon vanilla extract
- Cooking spray

Directions:

1. At 320°F, preheat your air fryer.
2. In a suitable mixing bowl, mix the almond flour, coconut flour, baking powder, pumpkin pie spice, and salt.
3. In another separate bowl, beat the eggs and Swerve until well combined. Add in the pumpkin puree, almond milk, and vanilla extract, and mix well.
4. Stir in the dry flour mixture and mix until well combined.
5. Grease a 7-inch baking pan or a cake pan that fits in your air fryer with cooking spray. Pour the prepared batter into the pan and smooth the top.
6. Place the pan in the air fryer basket and cook for 35 minutes. To check if it's done from the center, insert a clean toothpick into the bread, and if it comes out clean, then your bread is done.
7. Allow the air-fried bread to cool in the pan for 10 minutes, then transfer this bread to a wire rack and leave it to cool completely.
8. Enjoy your low-carb air fryer pumpkin bread!

Nutritional Information (76g per serving):

Calories: 182| Fat: 14 g| Sodium: 198 mg| Carbs: 8 g| Fiber: 4 g| Sugars: 2 g| Protein: 7 g

English Muffin

Prep time: 10 minutes. | **Cook time:** 15 minutes. | **Serves:** 6

Ingredients:

- ½ cup almond flour
- 2 tablespoons coconut flour
- ½ teaspoon baking powder
- ¼ teaspoon salt
- 2 tablespoons melted butter
- 2 eggs
- ¼ cup unsweetened almond milk
- Sesame seeds (optional)
- Cooking spray

Directions:

1. At 325°F, preheat your air fryer.
2. In a suitable mixing bowl, mix the almond flour, coconut flour, baking powder, and salt.
3. In another separate bowl, beat the eggs and add the melted butter and almond milk. Mix well.
4. Stir in dry flour mixture and mix until well combined.
5. Grease four silicone egg bite molds with cooking spray. Divide the prepared batter evenly among the molds and sprinkle with sesame seeds (optional).
6. Place these molds in the air fryer basket and air fry for 15 minutes.
7. To check if it's done from the center, insert a clean toothpick, and if it comes out clean, then your muffins are done.
8. Allow the muffins to cool in the molds for a few minutes, then remove them from the molds and let them cool completely on a wire rack.
9. Enjoy your low-carb air fryer English muffins!

Nutritional Information (80g per serving):

Calories: 144| Fat: 12 g| Sodium: 200 mg| Carbs: 4 g| Fiber: 2 g| Sugars: 1 g| Protein: 6 g

Apple Cobbler

Prep time: 10 minutes. | **Cook time:** 20 minutes. | **Serves:** 2

Ingredients:

- 2 medium apples, peeled and thinly sliced
- 1 tablespoon lemon juice
- 1/4 cup granulated Swerve
- 1 teaspoon ground cinnamon
- 1/4 teaspoon ground nutmeg
- 1/4 teaspoon salt
- 1/4 cup almond flour
- 1/4 cup coconut flour
- 1/4 cup unsalted butter, melted
- 2 tablespoons heavy cream
- 1/4 teaspoon vanilla extract
- 1/4 teaspoon baking powder
- 1/4 teaspoon xanthan gum

Directions:

1. At 375 °F, preheat your air fryer.
2. In a suitable mixing bowl, toss the apple slices with lemon juice, Swerve, cinnamon, nutmeg, and salt until the apples are coated.
3. In another mixing bowl, whisk together almond flour, coconut flour, melted butter, heavy cream, vanilla extract, baking powder, and xanthan gum until the mixture forms a dough-like consistency.
4. Divide the prepared apple mixture evenly among two ramekins.
5. Top each ramekin with the dough mixture, pressing it down lightly to cover the apples.
6. Place the ramekins in the preheated air fryer and cook for 15-18 minutes, or until the cobbler topping is golden brown and the apples are tender.
7. Serve the low carb air fryer apple cobbler warm, garnished with a pinch of cinnamon if desired.

Nutritional Information (107g per serving):
Calories 336| Fat: 28g | Sodium: 297mg | Carbs:21g | Fiber 7g | Sugar: 8g| Protein: 4g

Banana Churro Oatmeal

Prep time: 20 minutes. | **Cook time:** 10 minutes. | **Serves:** 4

Ingredients:

For the churros

- 1 large yellow banana, peeled, cut in half lengthwise, then cut in half widthwise
- 2 tablespoons whole-wheat pastry flour
- ⅛ teaspoon sea salt
- 2 teaspoons sunflower oil
- 1 teaspoon water
- Cooking spray
- 1 tablespoon coconut sugar
- ½ teaspoon cinnamon

For the oatmeal

- ¾ cup rolled oats
- 1½ cups water
- Non-dairy milk of your choice (optional)

Directions:

To make the churros

1. At 350 °F, preheat your air fryer for 5 minutes.
2. Place the 4 banana pieces in a suitable-sized bowl and add the flour and salt. Stir gently.
3. Add the sunflower oil and water. Stir gently until evenly mixed.
4. Spray the air fryer basket with the oil spray.
5. Place the banana pieces in the air fryer basket.
6. When the Unit is preheated, slide the basket in the air fryer and begin cooking for 10 minutes until done. Remove, gently turn over, and air fry for another 5 minutes.
7. In a suitable bowl, add the coconut sugar and cinnamon and stir to combine.
8. When the banana pieces are nicely browned, spray with the oil and place in the cinnamon-sugar bowl. Toss gently with a spatula to coat the banana pieces with the mixture.

To make the oatmeal

9. While the bananas are cooking, make your oatmeal. In a suitable pot, bring the oats

and water to a boil, then lower it to low heat.
10. Simmer, often stirring, until all of the water is absorbed, about 5 minutes. Place the oatmeal into two bowls.
11. If desired, pour a suitable amount of non-dairy milk on top.
12. Top your oatmeal with the coated banana pieces and serve immediately.
13. Enjoy with fresh berries on the side, if desired.

Nutritional Information (116 g per serving):
Calories 185| Fat: 3.6g | Sodium: 80mg | Carbs:17g | Fiber 3g | Sugar: 2g| Protein: 4g

Crunchy Breakfast Casserole

Prep time: 2 minutes. | **Cook time:** 30 minutes. | **Serves:** 2

Ingredients:
- 6 ounces of raw sweet sausage, remove from the casings
- 4 eggs
- ½ cup Whole bread crumbs
- 1 cup shredded cheddar cheese
- Black pepper and salt, to taste

Directions:
1. At 350 °F, preheat your air fryer.
2. Cook the raw sausage for 10 minutes on medium-to-high heat in a pan, breaking it up with a wooden spoon to prevent clumping. Remove and set aside.
3. Beat the eggs in a suitable mixing bowl, until light and fluffy. Stir in half of the bread crumbs, half of the cheese, the cooked sausage meat, black pepper and salt.
4. Pour into a baking dish and sprinkle the remaining bread crumbs and shredded cheese on top.
5. Place this baking dish in the air fryer basket, set the timer for 20 minutes.
6. Remove, serve and enjoy with low-carb bread of your choice.

Nutritional Information (180 g per serving):
Calories 364| Fat: 18g | Sodium: 370mg | Carbs:10g | Fiber 3g | Sugar: 2g| Protein: 21g

Thai Style Omelet

Prep time: 15 minutes. | **Cook time:** 10 minutes. | **Serves:** 2

Ingredients:
- 3½ ounces minced pork
- 2 eggs
- 1 cup onion, chopped
- 1 tablespoon fish salt

Directions:
1. At 280°F, preheat you air fryer.
2. Beat the eggs until you get a light and fluffy consistency.
3. In a bowl, add together all the recipe ingredients.
4. Pour the mixture into a baking pan then transfer it to the Air Fryer basket.
5. Air fry for 10 minutes or once omelet is golden brown. Cut and serve.
6. Enjoy with your favorite bread.

Nutritional Information (184g per serving):
Calories 315| Fat: 21g | Sodium: 134mg | Carbs:6g | Fiber 1g | Sugar: 3g| Protein: 23g

Cheesy Asparagus Frittata

Prep time: 15 minutes. | **Cook time:** 15 minutes. | **Serves:** 4

Ingredients:
- 1 cup asparagus spears, cut into 1-inch (2.5 cm) pieces
- 1 teaspoon vegetable oil
- 6 eggs
- 1 tablespoon milk
- 2 ounces goat cheese
- 1 tablespoon minced chives
- Black pepper and salt, to taste

Directions:
1. At 400 °F, preheat your air fryer.

2. Toss the asparagus pieces with the vegetable oil in a suitable bowl.
3. Place this asparagus in a 7-inch baking pan then transfer to the air fryer basket.
4. Air fry it for 5 minutes until the asparagus is softened and slightly wrinkled. Remove the pan.
5. Whisk the eggs with milk and pour the mixture over the asparagus in the pan.
6. Crumble cheese over the eggs and add the chives, if using. Season with black pepper and salt to taste.
7. Transfer this pan to the air fryer basket and air fry for 20 minutes, until the eggs are cooked through. Serve immediately.
8. Enjoy with your favorite bread.

Nutritional Information (177g per serving): Calories 282| Fat: 20g | Sodium: 259mg | Carbs:4g | Fiber 1g | Sugar: 3g| Protein: 19g

Egg, Bean and Mushroom Burrito

Prep time: 10 minutes. | **Cook time:** 15 minutes. | **Serves:** 2

Ingredients:

- 2 tablespoons canned black beans, rinsed and drained
- ¼ cup baby portobello mushrooms, sliced
- 1 teaspoon olive oil
- Pinch of salt
- 1 large egg
- 1 slice low-fat cheddar cheese
- 1 eight-inch whole grain flour tortilla
- ¼ cup hot sauce, to serve
- Cooking spray

Directions:

1. At 400 °F, preheat your air fryer.
2. Spray the air fryer pan with nonstick cooking spray, then place the black beans and baby portobello mushrooms in the pan, drizzle with the olive oil, and season with the salt.
3. Place the pan into the air fryer. Air fry for 5 minutes, then pause the fryer to crack the egg on top of the beans and mushrooms. Air fry for 8 more minutes until the egg is cooked as desired.
4. Pause the fryer again, top the eggs with cheese, and air fry for 1 minute.
5. Remove the pan from the fryer, then use a spatula to place this bean mixture on the whole grain flour tortilla. Fold in the sides and roll from front to back.
6. Serve warm with the hot sauce on the side.

Nutritional Information (97g per serving): Calories 226| Fat: 8g | Sodium: 121mg | Carbs:11g | Fiber 3g | Sugar: 2g| Protein: 11g

Omelet Cups with Bell Pepper and Onion

Prep time: 15 minutes. | **Cook time:** 10 minutes. | **Serves:** 2

Ingredients:

- 4 large eggs
- ½ bell pepper, finely chopped
- 1 tablespoon red onion, finely chopped
- ¼ teaspoon salt
- ¼ teaspoon black pepper
- 2 tablespoons shredded cheddar cheese
- Cooking spray

Directions:

1. At 400 °F, preheat your air fryer.
2. In a suitable bowl, mix well the eggs, then stir in the bell pepper, red onion, black pepper and salt.
3. Spray two 3-inch ramekins with nonstick cooking spray, then pour half the egg mixture into each ramekin and place the ramekins in the fryer basket. Place the basket into the air fryer, Air fry for 8 minutes.
4. Pause the fryer, sprinkle 1 tablespoon of shredded cheddar cheese on top of each cup, and air fry for 2 more minutes.
5. Remove the ramekins from the fryer and allow to cool on a wire rack for 5 minutes, then turn the omelet cups out on plates

and sprinkle some black pepper on top before serving.
6. Enjoy with a low-carb bread of your choice.

Nutritional Information (65g per serving): Calories 120| Fat: 9g | Sodium: 181mg | Carbs:4g | Fiber 0g | Sugar: 2g| Protein: 6g

Egg and Ham Casserole

Prep time: 10 minutes. | **Cook time:** 12 minutes. | **Serves:** 2

Ingredients:

- 1 cup day-old whole grain bread, cubed
- 3 large eggs, beaten
- 2 tablespoons water
- 1/8 teaspoon salt
- 1 ounce prosciutto, roughly chopped
- 1 ounce slice pepper jack cheese, chopped
- 1 tablespoon fresh chives, chopped
- Cooking spray

Directions:

1. At 400 °F, preheat your air fryer.
2. Spray a 7 inch baking pan with nonstick cooking spray, then place bread cubes in the pan.
3. In a suitable bowl, mix well the eggs and water, then stir in the salt, prosciutto, pepper jack cheese, and chives.
4. Then pour the prepared egg mixture on top of the bread cubes then air fry for 10–12 minutes until the eggs have set and the top is golden brown.
5. Remove the casserole from the fryer and allow to cool in the pan on a wire rack for 5 minutes before cutting and serving.
6. Slice and enjoy warm.

Nutritional Information (73g per serving): Calories 115| Fat: 8g | Sodium: 1184mg | Carbs:2g | Fiber 0g | Sugar: 1g| Protein: 8g

Egg Prosciutto

Prep time: 15 minutes. | **Cook time:** 8 minutes. | **Serves:** 2

Ingredients:

- 2 large eggs
- 2 slices of prosciutto
- Black pepper and salt, to taste

Directions:

1. At 350 °F, preheat your air fryer.
2. Take two 4 ounces ramekins and line each with a prosciutto slice.
3. Crack the eggs into the ramekins then transfer them to air fryer basket
4. Sprinkle Black pepper and salt, to taste on top.
5. Place this air fryer basket into the air fryer and air fry for 8 minutes.
6. Serve the eggs and prosciutto on a suitable plate.
7. Enjoy with your favorite bread.

Nutritional Information (69g per serving): Calories: 210| Fat: 14g| Sodium: 604 mg |Carbs: 1g|Fiber: 0g|Sugar: 1g| Protein: 20g

Egg Bites

Prep time: 10 minutes. | **Cook time:** 12 minutes. | **Serves:** 2

Ingredients:

- 4 large eggs
- ¼ cup shredded cheddar cheese
- ¼ cup diced ham
- ¼ cup diced bell peppers
- ¼ cup diced onions
- Black pepper and salt, to taste
- Cooking spray

Directions:

1. At 300 °F, preheat your air fryer.
2. In a suitable mixing bowl, beat the eggs together with the cheese, ham, bell peppers, onions, black pepper and salt.
3. Grease the wells of a silicone egg bite molds tray with cooking spray.

4. Pour the egg mixture into the mold, filling each well about 2/3 full.
5. Tap the mold gently on the counter to remove any air bubbles.
6. Place this mold into the air fryer basket and air fry for 12 minutes until the egg bites are set and slightly golden on top.
7. Carefully remove the mold from the air fryer and let the egg bites cool for a few minutes.
8. With a butter knife or spoon gently remove the egg bites from the mold.
9. Serve the egg bites warm and enjoy!

Nutritional Information (80g per serving):
Calories: 380| Fat: 25g| Sodium: 845mg| Carbs: 7g| Fiber: 1g| Sugars: 4g| Protein: 29g

Scotch Eggs

Prep time: 15 minutes. | **Cook time:** 20 minutes. | Serves: 4

Ingredients:

- 4 large hard-boiled eggs
- ½ lb ground pork sausage
- ½ teaspoon dried thyme
- ½ teaspoon dried sage
- ½ teaspoon paprika
- Black pepper and salt, to taste
- ¼ cup almond flour
- 1 large egg, beaten
- Cooking spray

Directions:

1. At 375 °F, preheat your air fryer.
2. Peel the hard-boiled eggs and set them aside.
3. In a suitable mixing bowl, combine the ground pork sausage, thyme, sage, paprika, black pepper and salt.
4. Make four equal portions of the sausage mixture.
5. Make a patty out of each portion and wrap it around one of the hard-boiled eggs, making sure to cover the entire egg.
6. In a shallow dish, whisk the beaten egg.
7. In another shallow dish, spread the almond flour.
8. Roll each sausage-wrapped egg in the beaten egg, then coat it with the almond flour.
9. Use a spritz of cooking spray to lightly grease your air fryer basket.
10. Place the sausage-wrapped eggs into the air fryer basket.
11. Spray the tops of the eggs with cooking spray.
12. Cook in the air fry for 20 minutes until the sausage is browned and cooked through.
13. Serve the Scotch eggs warm and enjoy!

Nutritional Information (100g per serving):
Calories: 340| Fat: 12g| Sodium: 550mg| Carbs: 5g| Fiber: 2g| Sugars: 1g| Protein: 26g

Broccoli Frittata

Prep time: 10 minutes. | **Cook time:** 15 minutes. | Serves: 4

Ingredients:

- 6 large eggs
- ½ cup chopped broccoli florets
- ¼ cup diced onions
- ¼ cup diced bell peppers
- ¼ cup shredded cheddar cheese
- Black pepper and salt, to taste
- Cooking spray

Directions:

1. At 350 °F, preheat your air fryer.
2. In a suitable mixing bowl, beat the eggs together with the broccoli, onions, bell peppers, cheese, black pepper and salt.
3. Spray a 7-inch round cake pan with cooking spray.
4. Pour the egg mixture into the pan.
5. Place the pan into the air fryer basket and air fry for 15 minutes until the frittata is set and slightly golden on top.
6. With a knife loosen the edges of the frittata, then invert it onto a suitable plate.
7. Serve the frittata in wedges while still warm.

8. Enjoy the frittata with low-carb bread of your choice.

Nutritional Information (90g per serving):
Calories: 300| Fat: 21g| Sodium: 470mg| Carbs: 6g| Fiber: 1g| Sugars: 2g| Protein: 21g

Egg Quiche

Prep time: 10 minutes. | **Cook time:** 20 minutes. | Serves: 4

Ingredients:

- 4 large eggs
- ½ cup heavy cream
- ¼ cup grated Parmesan cheese
- ¼ cup chopped spinach
- ¼ cup diced onions
- ¼ cup diced bell peppers
- ¼ cup diced ham
- Black pepper and salt, to taste
- Cooking spray

Directions:

1. At 350 °F, preheat your air fryer.
2. In a suitable mixing bowl, whisk the eggs together with the heavy cream, Parmesan cheese, black pepper and salt.
3. Spray a 7-inch round cake pan with cooking spray.
4. Spread the spinach, onions, bell peppers, and ham evenly over the bottom of the pan.
5. Pour the prepared egg mixture over the vegetables and meat.
6. Place the pan into the air fryer basket and air fry for 20 minutes until the quiche is set and slightly golden on top.
7. With a knife loosen the edges of the quiche, then invert it onto a suitable plate.
8. Serve the quiche warm, cut into wedges.

Nutritional Information (90g per serving):
Calories: 580| Fat: 48g| Sodium: 950mg| Carbs: 6g| Fiber: 1g| Sugars: 2g| Protein: 30g

Low-Carb Granola

Prep time: 10 minutes. | **Cook time:** 12 minutes. | Serves: 6

Ingredients:

- ½ cup chopped almonds
- ½ cup chopped pecans
- ½ cup unsweetened coconut flakes
- ¼ cup chia seeds
- ¼ cup flaxseed meal
- 2 tablespoons coconut oil, melted
- 1 tablespoon ChocZero maple syrup
- ½ teaspoon cinnamon
- ¼ teaspoon salt

Directions:

1. At 300 °F, preheat your air fryer.
2. In a suitable bowl, mix the chopped almonds, chopped pecans, unsweetened coconut flakes, chia seeds, flaxseed meal, cinnamon, and salt.
3. In a separate bowl, mix well the melted coconut oil and ChocZero maple syrup.
4. Pour the coconut oil and ChocZero maple syrup mixture over the nut mixture, and mix well.
5. Spread the mixture in a thin layer in a 7 inches pan then transfer to the air fryer basket.
6. Air fry for 12 minutes, stirring every 3-4 minutes, until the granola is crispy and golden.
7. Remove the air fried granola from the air fryer basket and let it cool.
8. Enjoy with fresh berries on the side.

Nutritional Information (80g per serving):
Calories: 306| Fat: 27g| Sodium: 98mg| Carbs: 15g| Fiber: 9g| Sugars: 4g| Protein: 7g

Low Carb Flat-Bread

Prep time: 15 minutes. | **Cook time:** 15 minutes. | **Serves:** 6

Ingredients:

- 1 cup almond flour
- ¼ cup coconut flour
- 2 tablespoons psyllium husk powder
- 1 teaspoon baking powder
- ¼ teaspoon salt
- 4 large eggs
- ¼ cup olive oil
- ¼ cup water
- Cooking spray

Directions:

1. At 380 °F, preheat your air fryer.
2. In a suitable mixing bowl, mix well the almond flour, coconut flour, psyllium husk powder, baking powder, and salt.
3. In a separate mixing bowl, mix well the eggs, olive oil, and water.
4. Stir in the dry flour mixture and mix well until a dough forms.
5. Knead the prepared dough for a few minutes until it becomes smooth.
6. Divide the prepared dough into four equal portions.
7. Roll each portion of your dough into a ball, then flatten it into a disc.
8. Use a spritz of cooking spray to lightly grease your air fryer basket.
9. Place the bread discs into the air fryer basket
10. Cook in the air fry for 15 minutes until golden brown.
11. Serve the bread warm and enjoy with eggs or bacon.

Nutritional Information (78g per serving):
Calories: 210| Fat: 18g| Sodium: 210mg| Carbs: 8g| Fiber: 5g| Sugars: 1g| Protein: 7g

Cauliflower Hash Brown

Prep time: 10 minutes. | **Cook time:** 12 minutes. | **Serves:** 4

Ingredients:

- 2 cups cauliflower florets, grated
- ¼ cup almond flour
- ¼ cup grated Parmesan cheese
- 1 egg
- ¼ teaspoon salt
- ¼ teaspoon black pepper
- ¼ teaspoon garlic powder
- Cooking spray

Directions:

1. At 375 °F, preheat your air fryer.
2. Place this grated cauliflower in a microwave-safe bowl and microwave for 3 minutes until tender.
3. Drain any excess liquid from the cauliflower and transfer it to a suitable mixing bowl.
4. Add almond flour, Parmesan cheese, egg, salt, black pepper, and garlic powder to the bowl with the cauliflower.
5. Mix the ingredients together until everything is well combined.
6. Use a spritz of cooking spray to lightly grease your air fryer basket.
7. Using a cookie scoop, drop the cauliflower mixture onto the air fryer basket, forming 6-8 hash browns.
8. Spray the hash browns with cooking spray.
9. Air fry for 12 minutes until the hash browns are crispy and golden brown.
10. Serve warm and enjoy with your favorite dipping sauce.

Nutritional Information (170g per serving):
Calories: 110| Fat: 7g| Sodium: 310mg| Carbs: 6g| Fiber: 2g| Sugars: 2g| Protein: 7g

Egg Zucchini Frittata

Prep time: 20 minutes. | **Cook time:** 12 minutes. | **Serves:** 4

Ingredients:

- 4 large eggs
- 1 medium zucchini, sliced
- ¼ cup grated Parmesan cheese
- ¼ cup chopped fresh parsley
- ¼ teaspoon garlic powder
- Black pepper and salt, to taste
- Cooking spray

Directions:

1. At 350 °F, preheat your air fryer.
2. In a suitable mixing bowl, whisk the eggs together with the Parmesan cheese, parsley, garlic powder, black pepper and salt.
3. Use a spritz of cooking spray to lightly grease your air fryer basket.
4. Spread the zucchini slices in one single layer in a baking pan and place it in the air fryer basket.
5. Pour the egg mixture over the zucchini slices.
6. Cook in the air fry for 12 minutes until the frittata is set and slightly golden on top.
7. Carefully remove the frittata from the air fryer.
8. With a knife loosen the edges of the frittata, then invert it onto a suitable plate.
9. Serve the frittata in wedges while still warm.
10. Enjoy with your favorite bread.

Nutritional Information (113g per serving):

Calories: 260| Fat: 17g| Sodium: 360mg| Carbs: 5g| Fiber: 1g| Sugars: 2g| Protein: 22g

Kuku Eggs

Prep time: 15 minutes. | **Cook time:** 12 minutes. | **Serves:** 2

Ingredients:

- 4 large eggs
- 1 small onion, finely chopped
- ½ cup chopped fresh parsley
- ½ cup chopped fresh cilantro
- ½ cup chopped fresh dill
- ¼ cup almond flour
- ½ teaspoon baking powder
- Black pepper and salt, to taste
- Cooking spray

Directions:

1. At 350 °F, preheat your air fryer.
2. In a suitable mixing bowl, whisk the eggs together with the almond flour, baking powder, black pepper and salt.
3. Stir in the chopped onion, parsley, cilantro, and dill.
4. Use a spritz of cooking spray to lightly grease a 7 inches baking pan.
5. Pour the egg mixture into the pan then transfer it to the air fryer basket.
6. Cook in the air fry for 12 minutes until the kuku is set and slightly golden on top.
7. With a knife loosen the edges of the kuku, then invert it onto a suitable plate.
8. Slice the kuku into wedges and serve warm.
9. Enjoy with your favorite bread.

Nutritional Information (113g per serving):

Calories: 275| Fat: 19g| Sodium: 365mg| Carbs: 10g| Fiber: 4g| Sugars: 2g| Protein: 19g

Chapter 4: Snacks

Chicken Samosa

Prep time: 15 minutes. | **Cook time:** 12 minutes. | **Serves:** 6

Ingredients:

- 1 pound ground chicken cooked
- ½ cup onion, chopped
- ½ cup carrots, grated
- ½ cup frozen peas
- ¼ cup fresh cilantro, chopped
- 1 teaspoon ground cumin
- 1 teaspoon ground coriander
- ½ teaspoon turmeric
- ½ teaspoon ground ginger
- ½ teaspoon salt
- ¼ teaspoon black pepper
- 20 egg roll wrappers
- Cooking spray

Directions:

1. At 375 °F, preheat your air fryer.
2. In a suitable bowl, mix the ground chicken or turkey, onion, carrots, peas, cilantro, cumin, coriander, turmeric, ginger, black pepper and salt.
3. Place one egg roll wrapper on a clean, dry surface, with one corner facing you. Spoon about 2 tablespoons of the chicken mixture onto the center of the wrapper.
4. Fold its corner closer to you over the filling, tucking it in tightly. Fold the left and right corners over the filling, and roll the wrapper away from you to seal the filling inside.
5. Repeat the same step with the remaining egg roll wrappers and filling.
6. Spray the samosas with cooking spray, and place them in one single layer in the air fryer basket.
7. Air fry for 12 minutes, until the samosas are golden brown and crispy.
8. Serve the samosas hot and enjoy with your favorite dipping sauce.

Nutritional Information (100g per serving):
Calories: 99| Fat: 2g| Sodium: 218mg| Carbs: 13g| Fiber: 1g| Sugars: 1g| Protein: 7g

Zucchini Fries

Prep time: 15 minutes. | **Cook time:** 12 minutes. | **Serves:** 4

Ingredients:

- 2 medium zucchinis, sliced into fries
- ½ cup almond flour
- ½ cup grated Parmesan cheese
- 1 teaspoon garlic powder
- 1 teaspoon onion powder
- ½ teaspoon salt
- ¼ teaspoon black pepper
- 2 eggs, beaten
- Cooking spray

Directions:

1. At 400 °F, preheat your air fryer.
2. In a shallow glass bowl, mix the almond flour, grated Parmesan cheese, garlic and onion powder, black pepper and salt.
3. Dip each zucchini fry into the beaten eggs, then coat it with the almond flour mixture.
4. Use a spritz of cooking spray to lightly grease your air fryer basket.
5. Place the coated zucchini fries in one single layer in the basket.
6. Air fry for 12 minutes, until the zucchini fries are golden brown and crispy, flip them halfway through.
7. Serve the zucchini fries hot and enjoy with your favorite dipping sauce.

Nutritional Information (113g per serving):
Calories: 303| Fat: 22g| Sodium: 710mg| Carbs: 11g| Fiber: 5g| Sugars: 3g| Protein: 17g

Cheese Puffs

Prep time: 15 minutes. | **Cook time:** 10 minutes. | **Serves:** 8

Ingredients:

- ½ cup almond flour
- ½ teaspoon baking powder
- ½ teaspoon garlic powder
- ½ teaspoon onion powder
- ¼ teaspoon salt
- ¼ teaspoon black pepper
- 2 eggs, beaten
- ½ cup shredded cheddar cheese
- Cooking spray

Directions:

1. At 350 °F, preheat your air fryer.
2. In a suitable bowl, mix the almond flour, baking powder, garlic and onion powder, black pepper and salt.
3. Add the beaten eggs and shredded cheddar cheese to the bowl, and stir until well combined.
4. Drop tablespoon-sized mounds of the mixture onto a suitable plate lined with parchment paper.
5. Use a spritz of cooking spray to lightly grease your air fryer basket.
6. Place the cheese puffs in one single layer in the basket.
7. Air fry for 10 minutes, until the cheese puffs are puffed and golden brown.
8. Serve the cheese puffs hot as a snack or appetizer.
9. Enjoy your cheese puffs with your favorite dip or sauce!

Nutritional Information (74g per serving):
Calories: 104| Fat: 8g| Sodium: 233mg|Carbs: 2g|Fiber: 1g|Sugar: 0g| Protein: 6g

Avocado Fries

Prep time: 10 minutes. | **Cook time:** 10 minutes. | **Serves:** 4

Ingredients:

- 2 ripe avocados, sliced into fries
- ½ cup almond flour
- ½ cup grated Parmesan cheese
- 1 teaspoon garlic powder
- ½ teaspoon salt
- ¼ teaspoon black pepper
- 2 eggs, beaten
- Cooking spray

Directions:

1. At 400 °F, preheat your air fryer.
2. In a shallow glass bowl, mix the almond flour, grated Parmesan cheese, garlic powder, black pepper and salt.
3. Dip each avocado fry into the beaten eggs, then coat it with the almond flour mixture.
4. Use a spritz of cooking spray to lightly grease your air fryer basket.
5. Place the coated avocado fries in one single layer in the basket.
6. Air fry for 10 minutes, until the avocado fries are golden brown and crispy, flip them halfway through.
7. Enjoy your avocado fries with your favorite dipping sauce!

Nutritional Information (70g per serving):
Calories: 345| Fat: 28g| Sodium: 651mg|Carbs: 15g| Fiber: 9g| Sugars: 1g| Protein: 13g

Pickle Fries

Prep time: 15 minutes. | **Cook time:** 10 minutes. | **Serves:** 4

Ingredients:
- 1 jar (16 ounces) dill pickle spears, drained and patted dry
- ½ cup almond flour
- ½ cup grated Parmesan cheese
- 1 teaspoon garlic powder
- ½ teaspoon paprika
- ½ teaspoon salt
- ¼ teaspoon black pepper
- 2 eggs, beaten
- Cooking spray

Directions:
1. At 400 °F, preheat your air fryer.
2. In a shallow glass bowl, mix the almond flour, grated Parmesan cheese, garlic powder, paprika, black pepper and salt.
3. Dip each pickle spear into the beaten eggs, then coat it with the almond flour mixture.
4. Use a spritz of cooking spray to lightly grease your air fryer basket.
5. Place the coated pickle spears in one single layer in the basket.
6. Air fry for 10 minutes, until the pickle fries are golden brown and crispy, flip them halfway through.
7. Enjoy your pickle fries with your favorite dipping sauce!

Nutritional Information (113g per serving):
Calories: 216|Fat: 16g| Sodium: 1509mg|Carbs: 10g|Fiber: 5g|Sugar: 0g| Protein: 12g

Kale Chips

Prep time: 10 minutes. | **Cook time:** 8 minutes. | **Serves:** 2

Ingredients:
- 1 bunch of kale, washed and dried
- 1 tablespoon olive oil
- ½ teaspoon salt

Directions:
1. At 300 °F, preheat your air fryer.
2. Remove the kale leaves from the stem and tear them into bite-sized pieces.
3. In a suitable bowl, toss the kale with olive oil and salt until evenly coated.
4. Spread the kale in the air fryer basket in a single layer.
5. Air fry for 6-8 minutes, until the kale chips are crispy and lightly browned, shaking the basket once cooked halfway through.
6. Remove the kale chips from the air fryer and transfer them to a serving bowl.
7. Serve the kale chips immediately as a healthy and delicious snack, with your favorite dipping sauce.

Nutritional Information (54g per serving):
Calories: 100|Fat: 7g | Sodium: 700mg |Carbs: 9g|Fiber: 3g|Sugars: 2g| Protein: 4g

Onion Rings

Prep time: 15 minutes. | **Cook time:** 12 minutes. | **Serves:** 4

Ingredients:
- 2 large onions, sliced into rings
- ½ cup almond flour
- ½ cup grated Parmesan cheese
- 1 teaspoon garlic powder
- ½ teaspoon paprika
- ½ teaspoon salt
- ¼ teaspoon black pepper
- 2 eggs, beaten
- Cooking spray

Directions:
1. At 400 °F, preheat your air fryer.
2. In a shallow glass bowl, mix the almond flour, grated Parmesan cheese, garlic powder, paprika, black pepper and salt.
3. Dip each onion ring into the beaten eggs, then coat it with the almond flour mixture.
4. Use a spritz of cooking spray to lightly grease your air fryer basket.
5. Place the coated onion rings in one single layer in the basket.
6. Air fry for 12 minutes, until the onion rings are golden brown and crispy, flip them halfway through.

7. Enjoy your onion rings with your favorite dipping sauce!

Nutritional Information (76g per serving):
Calories: 276|Fat: 18g| Sodium: 230mg |Carbs: 16g|Fiber: 4g|Sugar: 5g| Protein: 16g

Plantains Chips

Prep time: 10 minutes. | **Cook time:** 12 minutes. | Serves: 2

Ingredients:
- 2 ripe plantains
- 1 tablespoon olive oil
- ½ teaspoon garlic powder
- ½ teaspoon smoked paprika
- Black pepper and salt, to taste

Directions:
1. At 380 °F, preheat your air fryer.
2. Peel the plantains and slice them thinly.
3. In a suitable bowl, mix the olive oil, paprika, garlic powder, black pepper and salt.
4. Add the plantain slices to the bowl and toss to coat them evenly in the seasoning mixture.
5. Place the seasoned plantain slices in one single layer in the air fryer basket.
6. Air fry for 12 minutes, flip the plantain slices over halfway through, until they are crispy and golden brown.
7. Serve the plantains hot as a side dish or snack with your favorite dipping sauce.

Nutritional Information (240g per serving):
Calories: 184| Fat: 6.8g| Sodium: 159mg| Carbs: 32g| Fiber: 2.5g| Sugars: 15g| Protein: 1.6g.

Jalapeno Poppers

Prep time: 15 minutes. | **Cook time:** 10 minutes. | Serves: 6

Ingredients:
- 6 jalapeno peppers
- 4 ounces cream cheese, softened
- ½ cup shredded cheddar cheese
- ¼ cup almond flour
- ¼ teaspoon garlic powder
- ¼ teaspoon onion powder
- ¼ teaspoon salt
- ¼ teaspoon black pepper
- 2 eggs, beaten
- Cooking spray

Directions:
1. At 375 °F, preheat your air fryer.
2. Cut the peppers in half (lengthwise) and then remove their seeds and membranes.
3. In a suitable mixing bowl, mix the cream cheese, shredded cheddar cheese, almond flour, garlic and onion powder, black pepper and salt until well combined.
4. Stuff each jalapeno piece with the cheese mixture.
5. Dip each jalapeno popper into the beaten eggs, then coat it with a thin layer of almond flour.
6. Use a spritz of cooking spray to lightly grease your air fryer basket.
7. Place the jalapeno poppers in one single layer in the basket.
8. Air fry for 10 minutes, until the jalapeno poppers are golden brown and the cheese is melted, flip them halfway through.
9. Enjoy your jalapeno poppers with your favorite dipping sauce!

Nutritional Information (240g per serving):
Calories: 332| Fat: 23.4g| Sodium: 208mg| Carbs: 7.6g| Fiber: 2.7g| Sugars: 3.3g| Protein: 12.4g

Pepperoni Chips

Prep time: 15 minutes. | **Cook time:** 7 minutes. | Serves: 6

Ingredients:
- 20-30 slices of pepperoni
- Cooking spray

Directions:
1. At 400 °F, preheat your air fryer.
2. Place the pepperoni slices in one single layer in the air fryer basket.
3. Spray the pepperoni slices with cooking spray.
4. Air fry for 7 minutes, until the pepperoni slices are crispy and slightly browned.
5. Remove the pepperoni chips from the air fryer and transfer them to a suitable plate.

6. Serve the pepperoni chips as a crispy and delicious low carb snack.
7. Enjoy with your favorite dipping sauce

Nutritional Information (64g per serving):
Calories: 140| Fat: 11g| Sodium: 500mg| Carbs: 0-2g| Fiber: 0g| Sugars: 0g| Protein: 15g

Spicy Peanuts

Prep time: 10 minutes. | **Cook time:** 10 minutes. | **Serves:** 8

Ingredients:
- 2 cups raw peanuts
- 1 tablespoon olive oil
- 1 tablespoon chili powder
- 1 teaspoon garlic powder
- 1 teaspoon smoked paprika
- ½ teaspoon cumin
- ½ teaspoon salt
- ¼ teaspoon cayenne pepper (optional)

Directions:
1. At 350 °F, preheat your air fryer.
2. In a suitable mixing bowl, combine the raw peanuts, olive oil, chili powder, garlic powder, smoked paprika, cumin, salt, and cayenne pepper (if using). Toss the peanuts until they are evenly coated with the spice mixture.
3. Place the coated peanuts in the air fryer basket in a single layer.
4. Air fry for 10 minutes, shaking the basket once cooked halfway through, until the peanuts are golden brown and crispy.
5. Remove the spicy peanuts from the air fryer and let them cool completely.
6. Serve the spicy peanuts as a crunchy and flavorful snack.
7. Enjoy with your favorite sauce.

Nutritional Information (70g per serving): Calories 228| Fat 20g|Sodium 164mg| Carbs: 6.9g| Fiber 3.6g| Sugars 1.7g|Protein 9.7g

Chicken Nuggets

Prep time: 15 minutes. | **Cook time:** 12 minutes. | **Serves:** 2

Ingredients:
- 1 pound chicken breasts, boneless, skinless, cut into bite-sized pieces
- ½ cup almond flour
- ½ cup grated Parmesan cheese
- 1 teaspoon garlic powder
- 1 teaspoon paprika
- ½ teaspoon salt
- ¼ teaspoon black pepper
- 2 eggs, beaten
- Cooking spray

Directions:
1. At 400 °F, preheat your air fryer.
2. In a shallow glass bowl, mix the almond flour, grated Parmesan cheese, garlic powder, paprika, black pepper and salt.
3. Dip each chicken nugget into the beaten eggs, then coat it with the almond flour mixture.
4. Use a spritz of cooking spray to lightly grease your air fryer basket.
5. Place the coated chicken nuggets in one single layer in the basket.
6. Air fry for 12 minutes, until the chicken nuggets are golden brown and crispy, flip them halfway through.
7. Serve the chicken nuggets hot and enjoy with your favorite dipping sauce.

Nutritional Information (74g per serving):
Calories: 278| Fat: 14 g| Sodium: 630 mg| Carbs: 4 g| Fiber: 1 g| Sugars: 0 g| Protein: 34 g

Mozzarella Sticks

Prep time: 15 minutes. | **Cook time:** 7 minutes. | **Serves:** 8

Ingredients:

- 8 mozzarella string cheese sticks
- ½ cup almond flour
- ½ cup grated Parmesan cheese
- 1 teaspoon garlic powder
- ½ teaspoon onion powder
- ½ teaspoon dried oregano
- ¼ teaspoon salt
- ¼ teaspoon black pepper
- 2 eggs, beaten
- Cooking spray

Directions:

1. At 400 °F, preheat your air fryer.
2. Cut all the mozzarella string cheese sticks in half.
3. In a shallow glass bowl, mix the almond flour, grated Parmesan cheese, garlic and onion powder, dried oregano, black pepper and salt.
4. Dip each mozzarella stick half into the beaten eggs, then coat it with the almond flour mixture.
5. Use a spritz of cooking spray to lightly grease your air fryer basket.
6. Place the coated mozzarella sticks in one single layer in the basket.
7. Air fry for 7 minutes, until the mozzarella sticks are golden brown and the cheese is melted, flip them halfway through.
8. Serve the mozzarella sticks hot and enjoy with your favorite dipping sauce.

Nutritional Information (113g per serving):
Calories: 238| Fat: 17 g| Sodium: 542 mg| Carbs: 5 g| Fiber: 2 g| Sugars: 1 g| Protein: 18 g

Carrot Fries

Prep time: 10 minutes. | **Cook time:** 12 minutes. | **Serves:** 4

Ingredients:

- 4-5 large carrots, peeled and cut into thin sticks
- 1 tablespoon olive oil
- ½ teaspoon garlic powder
- ½ teaspoon paprika
- ¼ teaspoon salt
- ¼ teaspoon black pepper
- Optional: fresh parsley or other herbs for garnish

Directions:

1. At 375 °F, preheat your air fryer.
2. In a suitable mixing bowl, combine the carrot sticks, olive oil, garlic powder, paprika, black pepper and salt. Toss well to evenly coat the carrots with the seasoning.
3. Place the seasoned carrot sticks in the air fryer basket, making sure they are in one single layer and not touching each other. If needed, cook them in batches.
4. Cook the carrot fries for 12 minutes, shaking the basket every 3-4 minutes to ensure even cooking.
5. Once the carrot fries are crispy and golden brown, remove them from the air fryer and transfer them to a serving dish. Garnish with fresh parsley or other herbs, if desired.
6. Serve the carrot fries immediately while they are still hot and crispy.
7. Enjoy your delicious and healthy air fryer carrot fries with your favorite dipping sauce.

Nutritional Information (94g per serving):
Calories: 64| Fat: 4 g| Sodium: 165 mg| Carbs: 7 g| Fiber: 2 g| Sugars: 3 g| Protein: 1 g

Bacon Wrapped Avocado Wedge

Prep time: 20 minutes. | **Cook time:** 12 minutes. | **Serves:** 4

Ingredients:

- 2 ripe avocados, pitted and cut into wedges
- 4-6 slices of sugar-free bacon, cut in half
- 1 tablespoon olive oil
- ¼ teaspoon garlic powder
- ¼ teaspoon onion powder
- Black pepper and salt, to taste

Directions:

1. At 375 °F, preheat your air fryer.
2. In a suitable mixing bowl, combine the olive oil, garlic and onion powder, black pepper and salt.
3. Brush the avocado wedges with the seasoned oil mixture, making sure they are evenly coated.
4. Wrap each avocado wedge with a half slice of bacon, starting at the wide end and working towards the tip. Secure the bacon with a toothpick.
5. Arrange the bacon-wrapped avocado wedges in the air fryer basket in one single layer (without overlapping).
6. Cook the bacon-wrapped avocado wedges for 12 minutes, until crispy and golden brown. To ensure even cooking, flip them halfway through.
7. Once the bacon-wrapped avocado wedges are cooked, remove them from the air fryer and transfer them to a serving dish.
8. Serve the bacon-wrapped avocado wedges hot, garnished with fresh herbs if desired.
9. Enjoy your delicious and indulgent air fryer bacon-wrapped avocado wedges with your favorite dipping sauce.

Nutritional Information (100g per serving):
Calories: 306| Fat: 28 g| Sodium: 250 mg| Carbs: 9 g| Fiber: 7 g| Sugars: 1 g| Protein: 6 g

Bacon Wrapped Jalapeno Peppers

Prep time: 20 minutes. | **Cook time:** 12 minutes. | **Serves:** 12

Ingredients:

- 12 jalapeno peppers, halved lengthwise and seeded
- 6-8 slices of sugar-free bacon, cut in half
- 4 ounces cream cheese, softened
- ½ teaspoon garlic powder
- ½ teaspoon onion powder
- Black pepper and salt, to taste

Directions:

1. At 375 °F, preheat your air fryer.
2. In a suitable mixing bowl, combine the cream cheese, garlic and onion powder, black pepper and salt. Mix well.
3. Fill each jalapeno pepper half with a suitable spoonful of the cream cheese mixture.
4. Wrap each jalapeno piece with a half slice of bacon, making sure the bacon is tightly wrapped around the pepper. Secure the bacon with a toothpick.
5. Arrange the bacon-wrapped jalapeno peppers in the air fryer basket in one single layer (without overlapping).
6. Cook the bacon-wrapped jalapeno peppers for 12 minutes, until the bacon is golden brown. To ensure even cooking, flip them halfway through.
7. Once the bacon-wrapped jalapeno peppers are cooked, remove them from the air fryer and transfer them to a serving dish.
8. Serve the bacon-wrapped jalapeno peppers hot, garnished with fresh herbs if desired.
9. Enjoy your delicious and spicy air fryer bacon-wrapped jalapeno peppers with your favorite dipping sauce.

Nutritional Information (110g per serving):
Calories 91|Fat: 7.5g|Sodium: 615mg|Carbs: 1.6g|Fiber: 0.6g|Sugars: 0.6g|Protein: 4.5g

Eggplant Fries

Prep time: 15 minutes. | **Cook time:** 12 minutes. | **Serves:** 2

Ingredients:

- 1 large eggplant, cut into fry-shaped pieces
- ½ cup almond flour
- 2 eggs, beaten
- 1 cup panko breadcrumbs
- ¼ cup grated Parmesan cheese
- ½ teaspoon garlic powder
- ½ teaspoon onion powder
- ½ teaspoon dried basil
- ¼ teaspoon salt
- ¼ teaspoon black pepper
- Olive oil or cooking spray

Directions:

1. At 375 °F, preheat your air fryer.
2. Set up three bowls for your breading station. In the first bowl, add the flour. In the second bowl, add the beaten eggs. In the third bowl, mix the breadcrumbs, Parmesan cheese, garlic and onion powder, dried basil, black pepper and salt.
3. Dip each eggplant fry into the flour, shaking off any excess. Then, dip it into the egg, letting any excess drip off. Finally, coat it in the breadcrumb mixture,
4. Place the breaded eggplant fries in the air fryer basket in one single layer (without overlapping).
5. Spray the eggplant fries with olive oil or cooking spray to help them crisp up.
6. Cook the eggplant fries for 12 minutes, shaking the basket every 3-4 minutes to ensure even cooking.
7. Once the eggplant fries are crispy and golden brown, remove them from the air fryer and transfer them to a serving dish.
8. Enjoy your delicious and healthy air fryer eggplant fries with your favorite dipping sauce.

Nutritional Information (100g per serving):
Calories: 256| Fat: 3 g| Sodium: 442 mg| Carbs: 21 g| Fiber: 2 g| Sugars: 2 g| Protein: 8 g

Cassava Fries

Prep time: 10 minutes. | **Cook time:** 20 minutes. | **Serves:** 2

Ingredients:

- 1 large cassava (also known as yuca), peeled and cut into fry-shaped pieces
- 1 tablespoon olive oil
- ½ teaspoon garlic powder
- ½ teaspoon onion powder
- ¼ teaspoon paprika
- Black pepper and salt, to taste
- Cooking spray

Directions:

1. At 375 °F, preheat your air fryer.
2. In a suitable mixing bowl, mix well the olive oil, garlic and onion powder, paprika, black pepper and salt.
3. Toss the cassava fries in the seasoned oil mixture until they are evenly coated.
4. Place the cassava fries in the air fryer basket in one single layer (without overlapping).
5. Spray the cassava fries with cooking spray to help them crisp up.
6. Cook the cassava fries for 20 minutes, shaking the basket every 5 minutes.
7. Once the cassava fries are crispy and golden brown, remove them from the air fryer and transfer them to a serving dish.
8. Enjoy your delicious and crispy air fryer cassava fries with your favorite dipping sauce!

Nutritional Information (113g per serving):
Calories: 262| Fat: 4 g| Sodium: 119 mg| Carbs: 53 g| Fiber: 3 g| Sugars: 2 g| Protein: 2 g

Cauliflower Croquettes

Prep time: 15 minutes. | **Cook time:** 12 minutes. | **Serves:** 4

Ingredients:

- 1 head of cauliflower, small florets
- ½ cup almond flour
- 2 eggs, beaten
- ½ cup breadcrumbs
- ¼ cup grated Parmesan cheese
- ½ teaspoon garlic powder
- ½ teaspoon onion powder
- ¼ teaspoon dried basil
- Black pepper and salt, to taste
- Cooking spray

Directions:

1. At 375 °F, preheat your air fryer.
2. Cook the cauliflower florets in boiling water for 7 minutes, until they are tender. Drain and let cool.
3. In a suitable mixing bowl, mix well the flour, garlic and onion powder, dried basil, black pepper and salt.
4. In the first bowl, add the seasoned flour. In the second bowl, add the beaten eggs. Combine the breadcrumbs and Parmesan cheese in the third bowl.
5. Dip each cauliflower floret first in the seasoned flour, then in the beaten eggs, and then finally coat with the breadcrumb mixture, pressing the breadcrumbs onto the cauliflower to ensure its fully coated.
6. Place the breaded cauliflower croquettes in the air fryer basket in one single layer (without overlapping).
7. Spray the cauliflower croquettes with cooking spray to help them crisp up.
8. Cook the cauliflower croquettes for 12 minutes, shake every 3-4 minutes.
9. Once the cauliflower croquettes are crispy and golden brown, remove them from the air fryer and transfer them to a serving dish.

Nutritional Information (113g per serving):
Calories: 301| Fat: 13 g| Sodium: 562 mg| Carbs: 31 g| Fiber: 8 g| Sugars: 5 g| Protein: 17 g

Zucchini Fritters

Prep time: 15 minutes. | **Cook time:** 12 minutes. | **Serves:** 4

Ingredients:

- 2 medium zucchinis, grated
- ½ cup almond flour
- ¼ cup grated Parmesan cheese
- ¼ cup chopped fresh parsley
- 2 cloves garlic, minced
- 2 eggs, beaten
- ½ teaspoon salt
- ¼ teaspoon black pepper
- Cooking spray

Directions:

1. At 375 °F, preheat your air fryer.
2. Place this grated zucchini in a fine mesh strainer over a bowl and sprinkle with salt. Let it sit for 10 minutes to drain the excess liquid. Use paper towels to squeeze out any remaining liquid.
3. In a suitable mixing bowl, combine the almond flour, Parmesan cheese, parsley, garlic, eggs, black pepper and salt. Mix well.
4. Add the drained zucchini to the mixture and stir until well combined.
5. Use a cookie scoop or spoon to scoop the zucchini mixture into the air fryer basket in one single layer (without overlapping).
6. Spray the zucchini fritters with cooking spray to help them crisp up.
7. Cook the zucchini fritters for 12 minutes, flip them halfway through the cooking time, until they are crispy and golden brown.
8. Serve the zucchini fritters hot with your favorite dipping sauce.
9. Enjoy your delicious and healthy zucchini fritters!

Nutritional Information (113g per serving):
Calories: 195| Fat: 11 g| Sodium: 472 mg| Carbs: 13 g| Fiber: 5 g| Sugars: 4 g| Protein: 14 g

Bacon Wrapped Zucchini Fries

Prep time: 10 minutes. | **Cook time:** 15 minutes. | **Serves:** 4

Ingredients:

- 2 medium zucchinis, cut into fry-shaped pieces
- 6 strips of sugar-free bacon
- ½ teaspoon garlic powder
- ½ teaspoon onion powder
- Black pepper and salt, to taste
- Cooking spray

Directions:

1. At 375 °F, preheat your air fryer.
2. Wrap each zucchini fry with a strip of bacon, making sure to wrap it tightly around the zucchini.
3. In a suitable mixing bowl, mix well the garlic and onion powder, black pepper and salt.
4. Place the bacon-wrapped zucchini fries in the air fryer basket in one single layer (without overlapping).
5. Spray the zucchini fries with cooking spray to help them crisp up.
6. Sprinkle the seasoning mixture over the zucchini fries.
7. Cook the bacon-wrapped zucchini fries for 15 minutes, flip them halfway through, until they are crispy and the bacon is cooked through.
8. Once the bacon-wrapped zucchini fries are done, remove them from the air fryer and transfer them to a serving dish.
9. Serve the bacon-wrapped zucchini fries hot with your favorite dipping sauce.
10. Enjoy your delicious and healthy bacon wrapped zucchini fries!

Nutritional Information (130g per serving):
Calories: 195| Fat: 11 g| Sodium: 472 mg| Carbs: 13 g| Fiber: 5 g| Sugars: 4 g| Protein: 14 g

Cassava Croquettes

Prep time: 15 minutes. | **Cook time:** 35 minutes. | **Serves:** 4

Ingredients:

- 1 lb cassava, peeled and diced into small pieces
- ½ cup almond flour
- ¼ cup grated Parmesan cheese
- 2 cloves garlic, minced
- 2 eggs, beaten
- ½ teaspoon salt
- ¼ teaspoon black pepper
- Cooking spray

Directions:

1. At 375 °F, preheat your air fryer.
2. Cook the cassava pieces in boiling water for 20 minutes, until they are tender. Drain and let cool.
3. In a suitable mixing bowl, combine the almond flour, Parmesan cheese, garlic, eggs, black pepper and salt. Mix well.
4. Add the cooled cassava pieces to the mixture and mash with a fork until well combined.
5. Use a cookie scoop or spoon to scoop the cassava mixture into the air fryer basket in one single layer (without overlapping).
6. Spray the cassava croquettes with cooking spray to help them crisp up.
7. Cook the cassava croquettes for 15 minutes, flip them halfway through, until they are crispy and golden brown.
8. Serve the cassava croquettes hot with your favorite dipping sauce.

Nutritional Information (130g per serving):
Calories: 351| Fat: 9 g| Sodium: 494 mg| Carbs: 63 g| Fiber: 4 g| Sugars: 3 g| Protein: 8 g

Chapter 5: Poultry

Chicken Kiev

Prep time: 15 minutes. | **Cook time:** 20 minutes.
Serves: 4

Ingredients:

- 4 chicken breasts, boneless, skinless
- 4 tablespoons unsalted butter, softened
- 2 cloves garlic, minced
- 1 tablespoon chopped fresh parsley
- ½ teaspoon salt
- ¼ teaspoon black pepper
- ½ cup almond flour
- ½ cup grated parmesan cheese
- 2 large eggs, beaten
- Cooking spray

Directions:

1. At 400°F, preheat your air fryer.
2. Use any meat mallet to pound the chicken breasts to an even thickness of ½ inch.
3. In a suitable glass or plastic bowl, mix the butter, garlic, parsley, black pepper and salt until well combined.
4. Divide the prepared butter mixture into 4 equal parts.
5. Spoon one portion of the butter mixture onto the center of each chicken breast.
6. Fold the chicken over the butter mixture, tucking in the sides to form a tight seal.
7. In a shallow dish, mix the almond flour and grated parmesan cheese.
8. Dip each stuffed chicken breast in the beaten eggs, then dredge it in the almond flour mixture until well coated.
9. Coat the airfryer basket with cooking spray.
10. Transfer the stuffed chicken breasts to the air fryer basket without overlapping.
11. Air fry the stuffed chicken for 20 minutes until the chicken is golden.
12. Flip the chicken once cooked halfway.
13. Serve the chicken Kiev hot.

Nutritional Information (170g per serving):
Calories: 554| Fat: 36 g| Sodium: 962 mg| Carbs: 6 g| Fiber: 2 g| Sugars: 1 g| Protein: 51 g

Chicken Broccoli

Prep time: 10 minutes. | **Cook time:** 16 minutes.
Serves: 2

Ingredients:

- 2 boneless chicken breasts, skinless, (6 ounces each), cut into bite-sized pieces
- 2 cups broccoli florets
- 2 tablespoons olive oil
- 1 teaspoon garlic powder
- ½ teaspoon onion powder
- ½ teaspoon paprika
- ¼ teaspoon salt
- ¼ teaspoon black pepper
- Cooking spray

Directions:

1. At 375°F, preheat your air fryer.
2. In a suitable bowl, toss the chicken pieces with the garlic powder, olive oil, onion powder, paprika, black pepper and salt until well coated.
3. Make use of cooking spray to coat the air fryer basket.
4. Place the seasoned chicken in your air fryer basket in a single layer.
5. Cook the chicken for 10 minutes, flip halfway through until the chicken is cooked well and golden brown.
6. Remove the air-fried chicken from the air fryer and set it aside.
7. Spray the air fryer basket again with cooking spray.
8. Add the broccoli florets to the basket.
9. Cook the broccoli for 5-6 minutes, shaking the basket once cooked halfway through cooking until the broccoli is tender and lightly charred.
10. Serve the chicken and broccoli hot, garnished with chopped fresh herbs, if desired.

Nutritional Information (170g per serving):
Calories: 326| Fat: 22 g| Sodium: 359 mg| Carbs: 14 g| Fiber: 5 g| Sugars: 3 g| Protein: 23 g

Chicken Teriyaki

Prep time: 15 minutes. | **Cook time:** 12 minutes. | Serves: 4

Ingredients:

- 2 chicken breasts, boneless, skinless (6 ounces each)
- Black pepper and salt, to taste
- ¼ cup low-sodium soy sauce
- 1 tablespoon sesame oil
- 1 tablespoon ChocZero maple syrup
- 1 tablespoon rice vinegar
- 1 teaspoon garlic powder
- 1 teaspoon ground ginger
- 1 tablespoon xanthan gum
- 1 tablespoon water
- Sesame seeds and green onions, chopped for garnish

Directions:

1. At 400 °F, preheat your air fryer.
2. Season the chicken breasts liberally with black pepper and salt.
3. In a suitable bowl, mix well the soy sauce, sesame oil, ChocZero maple syrup, rice vinegar, garlic powder, and ground ginger.
4. Place the chicken breasts in the air fryer basket and air fry for 10 minutes, flip halfway through.
5. While the chicken is cooking, pour the sauce into a suitable saucepan and heat over medium-high heat.
6. In a suitable bowl, mix well the xanthan gum and water until smooth. Add the xanthan gum mixture to the saucepan and whisk to combine.
7. Bring the sauce to a boil and cook for 1-2 minutes, until thickened.
8. Brush the chicken breasts with the teriyaki sauce and cook for an additional 3 minutes, until the sauce is sticky and caramelized.
9. Garnish with sesame seeds and green onions.
10. Serve and enjoy your chicken teriyaki!

Nutritional Information (170g per serving):
Calories: 362| Fat: 14 g| Sodium: 1159 mg| Carbs: 21 g| Fiber: 1 g| Sugars: 14 g| Protein: 37 g

Stuffed Chicken Breast

Prep time: 15 minutes. | **Cook time:** 20 minutes. | Serves: 2

Ingredients:

- 2 chicken breasts, boneless, skinless (6 ounces each)
- Black pepper and salt, to taste
- ¼ cup cream cheese, softened
- ¼ cup grated Parmesan cheese
- 2 tablespoons chopped fresh basil
- 2 cloves garlic, minced
- ¼ cup almond flour
- ¼ cup grated mozzarella cheese
- 1 large egg, beaten
- Cooking spray

Directions:

1. At 375 °F, preheat your air fryer.
2. Cut a pocket into each chicken breast, being careful not to cut through to the other side.
3. Season the chicken breasts liberally with black pepper and salt.
4. In a suitable bowl, mix the cream cheese, Parmesan cheese, basil, and garlic until well combined.
5. Stuff the prepared chicken breasts with the cream cheese mixture.
6. In another glass bowl, mix the almond flour and grated mozzarella cheese.
7. Dip each stuffed chicken breast into the beaten egg, then coat it in the almond flour mixture.
8. Use a spritz of cooking spray to lightly grease your air fryer basket, then place the chicken breasts in the basket.
9. Air fry for 20 minutes, until golden brown and crispy.
10. Serve and enjoy your stuffed chicken breast!

Nutritional Information (200g per serving):
Calories: 525| Fat: 32g| Sodium: 710mg| Carbs: 11g| Fiber: 4g| Sugars: 3g| Protein: 51g

Dragon Chicken

Prep time: 15 minutes. | **Cook time:** 17 minutes. | **Serves:** 2

Ingredients:

For the chicken:

- 2 chicken breasts, boneless, skinless (6 ounces each)
- Black pepper and salt, to taste
- ¼ cup almond flour
- ¼ cup coconut flour
- 1 teaspoon garlic powder
- ½ teaspoon onion powder
- ½ teaspoon paprika
- ½ teaspoon salt
- ¼ teaspoon black pepper
- 1 large egg, beaten
- Cooking spray

For the dragon sauce:

- ¼ cup hot sauce (use a low-carb hot sauce if desired)
- 1 tablespoon butter
- 1 tablespoon ChocZero maple syrup
- 1 teaspoon soy sauce
- 1 teaspoon rice vinegar
- ½ teaspoon garlic powder

Directions:

1. At 400 °F, preheat your air fryer.
2. Cut all the chicken breasts into bite-sized pieces and season with black pepper and salt.
3. In a shallow glass bowl, mix the almond flour, coconut flour, garlic and onion powder, paprika, black pepper and salt.
4. Dip each chicken piece into the beaten egg, then coat it in the flour mixture.
5. Use a spritz of cooking spray to grease your air fryer basket, then place the chicken pieces in the basket.
6. Air fry for 15 minutes, shaking the basket once cooked halfway through, until the chicken is cooked well and the coating is crispy and golden brown.
7. While the chicken is cooking, make the dragon sauce. In a suitable saucepan, melt the butter over medium heat. Add the hot sauce, ChocZero maple syrup, soy sauce, rice vinegar, and garlic powder. Whisk to combine.
8. Bring the sauce to a simmer and cook it for 1-2 minutes, until slightly thickened.
9. Remove the air fried chicken from the air fryer basket and toss with the dragon sauce until well coated.
10. Serve and enjoy your dragon chicken!

Nutritional Information (240g per serving):
Calories: 475|Fat: 23g|Carbs: 14g|Fiber: 6g|Sugars: 8g| Protein: 46g

Chicken Meatloaf

Prep time: 15 minutes. | **Cook time:** 35 minutes. | **Serves:** 4

Ingredients:

- 1 lb ground chicken
- ½ cup almond flour
- ¼ cup grated Parmesan cheese
- ¼ cup chopped onion
- ¼ cup chopped celery
- ¼ cup chopped green pepper
- 1 tablespoon Worcestershire sauce
- 1 teaspoon garlic powder
- 1 teaspoon dried thyme
- ½ teaspoon salt
- ¼ teaspoon black pepper
- 1 large egg, beaten
- Cooking spray

Directions:

1. At 350 °F, preheat your air fryer.
2. In a suitable bowl, mix the ground chicken, almond flour, Parmesan cheese, onion, celery, green pepper, Worcestershire sauce, garlic powder, thyme, salt, pepper, and beaten egg until well combined.
3. Grease a suitable loaf pan with cooking spray, then transfer the meat mixture to the pan, pressing it down to make sure it's evenly distributed.
4. Place the loaf pan with meatloaf in your air fryer basket.

5. Air fry for 35 minutes, until golden brown.
6. Remove the loaf pan from the air fryer basket and let the meatloaf cool for a few minutes before slicing and serving.
7. Serve and enjoy your chicken meatloaf!

Nutritional Information (170g per serving):
Calories: 274|Fat: 16g| Sodium: 666mg|Carbs: 7g|Fiber: 3g|Sugar: 2g| Protein: 25g

Chicken Tenders

Prep time: 15 minutes. | **Cook time:** 10 minutes. | Serves: 4

Ingredients:

- 1 lb chicken breasts, boneless, skinless cut into strips
- ½ cup almond flour
- ½ teaspoon garlic powder
- ½ teaspoon onion powder
- ½ teaspoon paprika
- ½ teaspoon salt
- ¼ teaspoon black pepper
- 1 large egg, beaten
- Cooking spray

Directions:

1. At 400 °F, preheat your air fryer.
2. In a shallow glass bowl, mix the almond flour with garlic and onion powder, paprika, black pepper and salt.
3. Dip each chicken strip into the beaten egg, then coat it in the almond flour mixture.
4. Use a spritz of cooking spray to lightly grease your air fryer basket, then place the chicken strips in the basket, leaving some space between each one.
5. Air fry for 10 minutes, flip the chicken strips halfway through, until the chicken is cooked well and the coating is crispy and golden brown.
6. Remove the air fried chicken strips from the air fryer basket and let them cool for a few minutes before serving.
7. Serve and enjoy your chicken tenders!

Nutritional Information (100g per serving):
Calories: 345| Fat: 16g| Sodium: 520mg| Carbs: 6g| Fiber: 3g| Sugars: 1g| Protein: 43g

Spinach Stuffed Chicken

Prep time: 10 minutes. | **Cook time:** 25 minutes. | Serves: 4

Ingredients:

- 4 chicken breasts, boneless, skinless (6 ounces each)
- 4 slices of prosciutto
- ½ cup of spinach leaves
- ½ cup of shredded mozzarella cheese
- ½ teaspoon of garlic powder
- ½ teaspoon of dried oregano
- Black pepper and salt, to taste
- Cooking spray

Directions:

1. At 380 °F, preheat your air fryer.
2. Butterfly the chicken breasts by slicing them horizontally, but not all the way through, and open them up like a book.
3. Place one slice of prosciutto, some spinach leaves, and shredded mozzarella cheese on one half of each chicken breast.
4. Sprinkle garlic powder, dried oregano, black pepper and salt on top of the stuffing.
5. Fold the other half of the chicken breast over the stuffing and secure with toothpicks.
6. Use a spritz of cooking spray to lightly grease your air fryer basket, then place the stuffed chicken breasts in the basket.
7. Air fry for 25 minutes, flip the chicken breasts halfway through, until the chicken is cooked well and the cheese is melted and bubbly.
8. Serve and enjoy your stuffed chicken!

Nutritional Information (180g per serving):
Calories: 536 |Fat: 20g| Sodium: 711mg |Carbs: 2g|Fiber: 1g| Protein: 35g

Bacon Wrapped Chicken

Prep time: 15 minutes. | **Cook time:** 25 minutes. | **Serves:** 4

Ingredients:

- 4 chicken breasts, skinless, boneless (6 ounces each)
- 8 slices of sugar-free bacon
- 1 teaspoon of garlic powder
- 1 teaspoon of smoked paprika
- ½ teaspoon of salt
- ¼ teaspoon of black pepper
- Cooking spray

Directions:

1. At 380 °F, preheat your air fryer.
2. Season the chicken breasts with garlic powder, smoked paprika, black pepper and salt.
3. Wrap each of the chicken breasts with 2 slices of bacon, tucking the ends under the chicken.
4. Use a spritz of cooking spray to lightly grease your air fryer basket, then place the bacon-wrapped chicken breasts in the basket.
5. Air fry for 25 minutes, flip the chicken breasts halfway through, until the chicken is cooked well and the bacon is crispy.
6. Remove the air fried chicken breasts from the air fryer basket and let them cool for a few minutes before serving.
7. Serve and enjoy your bacon wrapped chicken!

Nutritional Information (190g per serving):
Calories: 682| Fat: 36g| Sodium: 1307mg| Carbs: 1g| Fiber: 0g| Sugars: 0g| Protein: 84g

Chicken Breast Asparagus Rolls

Prep time: 10 minutes. | **Cook time:** 20 minutes. | **Serves:** 2

Ingredients:

- 4 chicken breasts, boneless, skinless (6 ounces each)
- 16 asparagus spears
- 8 slices of prosciutto
- 2 tablespoons of olive oil
- 1 teaspoon of garlic powder
- 1 teaspoon of dried thyme
- Black pepper and salt, to taste
- Cooking spray

Directions:

1. At 375 °F, preheat your air fryer.
2. Season the chicken breasts with olive oil, garlic powder, dried thyme, black pepper and salt.
3. Lay out a slice of prosciutto and place 2 asparagus spears on top.
4. Place a chicken breast on top of the asparagus, then roll the prosciutto tightly around the chicken and asparagus.
5. Repeat with the remaining chicken breasts, asparagus, and prosciutto.
6. Use a spritz of cooking spray to lightly grease your air fryer basket, then place the chicken and asparagus rolls in the basket.
7. Air fry for 18-20 minutes, flip the rolls halfway through, until the chicken is cooked well and the prosciutto is crispy.
8. Remove the chicken and asparagus rolls from the air fryer basket and let them cool for a few minutes before serving.
9. Serve and enjoy your air fryer chicken breast asparagus rolls!

Nutritional Information (200g per serving):
Calories: 396| Fat: 22g| Sodium: 736mg| Carbs: 4g| Fiber: 2g| Sugars: 1g| Protein: 45g

Chicken Drumsticks

Prep time: 15 minutes. | **Cook time:** 25 minutes. | **Serves:** 4

Ingredients:

- 8 chicken drumsticks
- 2 tablespoons of olive oil
- 1 teaspoon of garlic powder
- 1 teaspoon of paprika
- ½ teaspoon of onion powder
- ½ teaspoon of dried thyme
- ½ teaspoon of dried basil
- Black pepper and salt, to taste
- Cooking spray

Directions:

1. At 400 °F, preheat your air fryer.
2. Season the chicken drumsticks with olive oil, garlic powder, paprika, onion powder, dried thyme, dried basil, black pepper and salt.
3. Use a spritz of cooking spray to lightly grease your air fryer basket, then place the chicken drumsticks in the basket.
4. Air fry for 25 minutes, flip the chicken drumsticks halfway through, until the chicken is cooked well and the skin is crispy.
5. Remove the chicken drumsticks from the air fryer basket and let them cool for a few minutes before serving.
6. Serve and enjoy your chicken drumsticks!

Nutritional Information (170g per serving):
Calories: 271| Fat: 18.5g| Sodium: 289mg| Carbs: 1.4g|Fiber: 0.5g|Sugar: 0.1g| Protein: 23.8g

Tandoori Chicken

Prep time: 15 minutes. | **Cook time:** 25 minutes. | **Serves:** 2

Ingredients:

- 4 chicken drumsticks
- ½ cup plain Greek yogurt
- 1 tablespoon lemon juice
- 1 tablespoon ginger paste
- 1 tablespoon garlic paste
- 2 teaspoons paprika
- 2 teaspoons ground cumin
- 1 teaspoon ground coriander
- ½ teaspoon turmeric powder
- ½ teaspoon garam masala
- Salt to taste
- Cooking spray

Directions:

1. In a suitable mixing bowl, combine Greek yogurt, lemon juice, ginger paste, garlic paste, paprika, ground cumin, ground coriander, turmeric powder, garam masala, and salt to taste.
2. Mix the ingredients well to form a marinade.
3. Add chicken drumsticks to the marinade and coat them well.
4. Cover this bowl with a plastic wrap and marinate this chicken in the refrigerator for 30 minutes or up to 4 hours.
5. Remove the refrigerated chicken from the marinade and shake off the excess marinade.
6. At 400 °F, preheat your air fry.
7. Use a spritz of cooking spray to lightly grease your air fryer basket.
8. Place the chicken drumsticks in the air fryer basket in a single layer.
9. Cook the chicken for 20 minutes, flip them halfway through the cooking time.
10. Once cooked, remove the chicken from the air fryer.
11. Enjoy with low-carb tortillas.

Nutritional Information (150g per serving):
Calories: 522|Fat: 35g| Sodium: 196mg|Carbs: 8g|Fiber: 2g|Sugar: 4g| Protein: 42g

Chicken Mushroom Skewers

Prep time: 10 minutes. | **Cook time:** 12 minutes. | **Serves:** 4

Ingredients:

- 2 boneless, chicken breasts (6 ounces each), skinless, cut into cubes
- 8-10 small mushrooms, cleaned and trimmed
- 1 tablespoon olive oil
- 1 tablespoon lemon juice
- 1 teaspoon garlic powder
- 1 teaspoon dried thyme
- Black pepper and salt, to taste
- Skewers

Directions:

1. At 400 °F, preheat your air fryer.
2. In a suitable bowl, mix well the olive oil, lemon juice, garlic powder, thyme, black pepper and salt.
3. Thread the chicken and mushroom onto the skewers, alternating them.
4. Brush the skewers with the olive oil mixture.
5. Place the skewers in the air fryer basket and air fry for 12 minutes, flip them halfway through, until the chicken is cooked well and the mushrooms are tender.
6. Serve hot and enjoy with your favorite salad.

Nutritional Information (200g per serving):
Calories: 197|Fat: 8.6 g| Carbs: 4.8 g| Fiber: 1.3 g| Sugars: 3.5 g| Protein: 25.6 g

Chicken Satay

Prep time: 15 minutes. | **Cook time:** 10 minutes. | **Serves:** 2

Ingredients:

- 1 lb chicken breasts, boneless, skinless, cut into strips
- 2 tablespoons coconut milk
- 2 tablespoons soy sauce
- 1 tablespoon ChocZero maple syrup
- 1 tablespoon peanut butter
- 1 tablespoon lime juice
- 1 garlic clove, minced
- ½ teaspoon ground cumin
- ¼ teaspoon ground coriander

Directions:

1. In a suitable bowl, mix well the coconut milk, soy sauce, ChocZero maple syrup, peanut butter, lime juice, garlic, cumin, and coriander to make the marinade.
2. Add the chicken strips to the bowl with the marinade and toss to coat.
3. Cover this bowl with plastic wrap and refrigerate for at least 30 minutes.
4. At 400 °F, preheat your air fryer.
5. Thread the prepared chicken strips onto the skewers and transfer them to your air fryer basket, leaving a little space between each skewer.
6. Air fry for 10 minutes, flip the skewers halfway through, until the chicken is cooked well and browned on the outside.
7. Serve the chicken satay skewers hot with additional peanut sauce or lime wedges for squeezing over the top.

Nutritional Information (170g per serving):
Calories: 358|Fat: 13.7g|Carbs: 12.9g|Fiber: 1.3g|Sugar: 8.2g| Protein: 41.3g

Chicken Fajita

Prep time: 20 minutes. | **Cook time:** 10 minutes. | **Serves:** 2

Ingredients:

- 1 lb chicken breasts, boneless, skinless, cut into strips
- 1 green bell pepper, sliced
- 1 red bell pepper, sliced
- 1 small onion, sliced
- 1 tablespoon olive oil
- 1 teaspoon chili powder
- ½ teaspoon garlic powder
- ½ teaspoon paprika
- ½ teaspoon cumin
- Black pepper and salt, to taste
- Fresh cilantro, chopped, for garnish

Directions:

1. At 400 °F, preheat your air fryer.
2. In a suitable bowl, mix well the olive oil, chili powder, garlic powder, paprika, cumin, black pepper and salt.
3. Add the chicken strips, bell peppers, and onion to the bowl with the olive oil mixture and toss to coat.
4. Place the chicken and vegetable mixture in the air fryer basket in a single layer.
5. Air fry for 10 minutes, shaking the basket once cooked halfway through, until the chicken is cooked well and the vegetables are tender and lightly charred.
6. Serve the low-carb chicken fajitas hot, garnished with chopped cilantro.
7. Enjoy with low-carb tortillas.

Nutritional Information (150g per serving):
Calories: 404| Fat: 14.7 g| Sodium: 520 mg| Carbs: 10.9 g| Fiber: 3.1 g| Sugars: 5.2 g| Protein: 57.5 g

Chicken Cordon Blue

Prep time: 10 minutes. | **Cook time:** 20 minutes. | **Serves:** 4

Ingredients:

- 4 chicken breasts, boneless, skinless (6 ounces each)
- 4 slices deli ham
- 4 slices Swiss cheese
- ½ cup almond flour
- ½ cup grated parmesan cheese
- 1 teaspoon garlic powder
- 1 teaspoon paprika
- ½ teaspoon salt
- ¼ teaspoon black pepper
- 2 eggs, beaten

Directions:

1. At 375 °F, preheat your air fryer.
2. Place each of the chicken breasts in between two pieces of plastic sheets and pound them with a meat mallet until they are an even thickness.
3. Add a slice of ham and a slice of Swiss cheese on each chicken breast, then fold the chicken in half to enclose the filling.
4. In a shallow dish, mix the almond flour, grated parmesan cheese, garlic powder, paprika, black pepper and salt.
5. Dip the chicken breasts in the beaten eggs, then dredge in the almond flour mixture, pressing the coating.
6. Place the chicken breasts in the air fryer basket, leaving a little space between them.
7. Air fry for 18-20 minutes, flip the chicken halfway through, until the chicken is cooked well and the coating is golden.
8. Let the cooked chicken rest for a few minutes before slicing and serving.
9. Enjoy with your favorite salad.

Nutritional Information (180g per serving):
Calories: 404| Fat: 14.7 g| Sodium: 520 mg| Carbs: 10.9 g| Fiber: 3.1 g| Sugars: 5.2 g| Protein: 57.5 g

Stuffed Turkey Rolls

Prep time: 20 minutes. | **Cook time:** 15 minutes. | **Serves:** 4

Ingredients:

- 4 thin turkey cutlets (6 ounces each)
- 4 slices prosciutto
- 4 slices provolone cheese
- ¼ cup chopped sun-dried tomatoes
- 2 tablespoons chopped fresh basil
- 1 tablespoon olive oil
- ½ teaspoon garlic powder
- ½ teaspoon dried oregano
- Black pepper and salt, to taste

Directions:

1. At 400 °F, preheat your air fryer.
2. Place each turkey cutlet between 2 pieces of plastic sheet and pound them with a meat mallet until they are an even thickness.
3. Lay a slice of prosciutto on each turkey cutlet, then top with a slice of provolone cheese.
4. In a suitable bowl, mix the chopped sun-dried tomatoes, fresh basil, olive oil, garlic powder, dried oregano, black pepper and salt.
5. Spoon the tomato mixture over the cheese, dividing it evenly among the turkey cutlets.
6. Roll up each turkey cutlet and secure with toothpicks.
7. Place the turkey rolls in the air fryer basket, leaving a little space between them.
8. Air fry for 15 minutes, flip the rolls halfway through, until the turkey is cooked well and the cheese is melted and bubbly.
9. Remove the toothpicks and serve the low-carb stuffed turkey rolls hot.
10. Enjoy with your favorite dipping sauce.

Nutritional Information (200g per serving):
Calories: 445| Fat: 23g| Sodium: 969mg| Carbs: 7g| Fiber: 1g| Sugars: 3g| Protein: 52g

Stuffed Whole Chicken

Prep time: 15 minutes. | **Cook time:** 70 minutes. | **Serves:** 8

Ingredients:

- 1 whole chicken, about 3-4 pounds
- 2 tablespoons butter
- ½ onion, diced
- 2 cloves garlic, minced
- ¼ cup chopped fresh parsley
- ¼ cup chopped fresh basil
- ¼ cup chopped fresh thyme
- 1 teaspoon paprika
- 1 teaspoon salt
- ½ teaspoon black pepper

Directions:

1. At 350 °F, preheat your air fryer.
2. In a suitable saucepan, melt the butter over medium heat.
3. Stir in the diced onion and minced garlic and cook for 5 minutes.
4. Remove this pan from the heat and stir in the chopped parsley, basil, and thyme.
5. Season the chicken inside and out with the paprika, black pepper and salt.
6. Stuff the chicken with the herb and onion mixture.
7. Tie both the chicken legs together with kitchen twine.
8. Transfer this whole chicken to the air fryer basket, breast side up.
9. Air fry for 60-70 minutes, until the chicken is cooked well and the internal temperature reaches 165°F (74°C).
10. Let the cooked chicken rest for a few minutes before carving and serving.
11. Enjoy your delicious and healthy air fryer low-carb stuffed whole chicken!

Nutritional Information (226g per serving):
Calories: 248 per serving| Fat: 15.4g| Sodium: 390mg| Carbs: 1.6g| Fiber: 0.4g| Sugars: 0.3g| Protein: 25.6g

Pesto Chicken

Prep time: 10 minutes. | **Cook time:** 20 minutes. | **Serves:** 4

Ingredients:

- 4 chicken breasts, boneless, skinless (6 ounces each)
- ½ cup basil pesto
- Black pepper and salt, to taste

Directions:

1. At 375 °F, preheat your air fryer.
2. Rub the chicken breasts liberally with black pepper and salt.
3. Spread a generous amount of pesto on each chicken breast, covering the top and sides.
4. Place the chicken breasts in the air fryer basket, leaving a little space between them.
5. 20 minutes in the air fryer will get the chicken cooked through.
6. Let the cooked chicken rest for a few minutes before slicing and serving.
7. Enjoy your delicious and easy air fryer pesto chicken!

Nutritional Information (170g per serving):
Calories: 640|Fat: 44g| Sodium: 550mg | Carbs: 10g |Fiber: 1g|Sugar: 1g| Protein: 56g

Chicken Parmesan

Prep time: 20 minutes. | **Cook time:** 15 minutes. | **Serves:** 4

Ingredients:

- 4 chicken breasts, boneless, skinless (6 ounces each)
- 1 cup almond flour
- ½ cup grated parmesan cheese
- ½ cup low-carb marinara sauce
- 1 cup shredded mozzarella cheese
- 1 teaspoon garlic powder
- 1 teaspoon Italian seasoning
- Black pepper and salt, to taste
- 2 eggs, beaten
- Fresh basil, chopped, for garnish (optional)

Directions:

1. At 375 °F, preheat your air fryer.
2. In a shallow dish, mix the almond flour, grated parmesan cheese, garlic powder, Italian seasoning, black pepper and salt.
3. In another shallow dish, beat the eggs.
4. Dip chicken in the beaten eggs, then coat in the almond flour mixture, pressing to adhere.
5. Place the chicken breasts in the air fryer basket, leaving a little space between them.
6. Air fry for 12 minutes, flip the chicken halfway through.
7. Spoon a little marinara sauce on each chicken breast, then sprinkle with shredded mozzarella cheese.
8. Air fry for an additional 3 minutes, until the cheese is melted and bubbly.
9. Garnish with fresh chopped basil, if desired, and serve hot.
10. Enjoy your delicious and healthy chicken parmesan!

Nutritional Information (200g per serving):
Calories: 581| Fat: 35 g| Sodium: 1097 mg| Carbs: 9 g| Fiber: 4 g| Sugars: 2 g| Protein: 57 g

Chicken Casserole

Prep time: 20 minutes. | **Cook time:** 15 minutes. | **Serves:** 2

Ingredients:

- 1 pound chicken breasts, boneless, skinless, cubed
- 1 tablespoon olive oil
- ½ onion, diced
- 2 cloves garlic, minced
- 1 red bell pepper, diced
- 1 yellow bell pepper, diced
- ½ cup chicken broth
- ½ cup heavy cream
- ½ cup grated parmesan cheese
- 1 cup shredded mozzarella cheese

- 1 teaspoon paprika
- 1 teaspoon dried thyme
- Black pepper and salt, to taste
- Fresh parsley, chopped, for garnish (optional)

Directions:

1. At 375 °F, preheat your air fryer.
2. In a suitable skillet, heat the olive oil over medium-high heat for 30 seconds.
3. Add the chicken cubes and air fry for 5-6 minutes, until browned on all sides.
4. Add the diced onion, minced garlic, red and yellow bell peppers, paprika, thyme, black pepper and salt. Air fry for an additional 3 minutes, until the vegetables are tender.
5. Pour the broth into the skillet and scrape up the browned bits.
6. Stir in cream and grated parmesan cheese. Stir to combine.
7. Transfer the chicken and vegetable mixture to an air fryer-safe casserole dish.
8. Top with shredded mozzarella cheese.
9. Air fry for 10 minutes, until the cheese is melted and bubbly.
10. Garnish with parsley and serve hot.
11. Enjoy your delicious and healthy chicken casserole!

Nutritional Information (190g per serving):
Calories: 452|Fat: 28g| Sodium: 708mg|Carbs: 9g|Fiber: 2g|Sugar: 4g| Protein: 42g

Herbed Turkey Breast

Prep time: 10 minutes. | **Cook time:** 25 minutes. | **Serves:** 6

Ingredients:

- 2-3 pounds boneless turkey breast
- 1 tablespoon olive oil
- 1 teaspoon dried thyme
- 1 teaspoon dried rosemary
- 1 teaspoon dried sage
- Black pepper and salt, to taste

Directions:

1. At 375 °F, preheat your air fryer.
2. In a suitable bowl, mix the olive oil, thyme, rosemary, sage, black pepper and salt.
3. Rub the prepared herb mixture all over the turkey breast.
4. Place the turkey breast in the air fryer basket.
5. Air fry for 25 minutes per pound.
6. Let the turkey breast rest for a few minutes before slicing and serving.
7. Enjoy with your favorite salad.

Nutritional Information (230g per serving):
Calories: 125|Fat: 1g| Sodium: 320mg |Carbs: 0g|Fiber: 1.2g| Sugars: 2g| Protein: 26g

Duck Breast Fillet

Prep time: 15 minutes. | **Cook time:** 20 minutes. | **Serves:** 2

Ingredients:

- 2 duck breast fillets (6 ounces each)
- 1 teaspoon salt
- ½ teaspoon black pepper
- ½ teaspoon garlic powder
- ½ teaspoon onion powder
- ½ teaspoon paprika

Directions:

1. At 375 °F, preheat your air fryer.
2. Season the duck breast fillets with salt, black pepper, garlic and onion powder, and paprika. Rub the spices all over the duck breasts.
3. Place the seasoned duck breasts in the air fryer basket, skin side down.
4. Cook the duck breasts for 10 minutes.
5. Flip the duck breasts over and air fry for an additional 10 minutes, until the internal temperature of the duck reaches 145°F.
6. Slice and enjoy with your favorite salad.

Nutritional Information (170g per serving):
Calories: 516|Fat: 38g| Sodium: 410mg |Carbs: 1g|Fiber: 2.2g| Sugars: 1g | Protein: 40g

Chapter 6: Seafood

Teriyaki Shrimp

Prep time: 10 minutes. | **Cook time:** 6 minutes.
Serves: 4

Ingredients:

- 1 pound raw shrimp, peeled and deveined
- ¼ cup sugar-free soy sauce
- 2 tablespoons choc Zero maple syrup
- 2 tablespoons rice vinegar
- 1 tablespoon sesame oil
- 1 teaspoon minced garlic
- 1 teaspoon minced ginger
- 1 tablespoon xanthan gum
- ¼ cup water
- Black pepper and salt, to taste
- Sesame seeds and green onions, sliced for garnish

Directions:

1. At 400°F, preheat your air fryer.
2. In a suitable mixing bowl, mix the soy sauce, choc Zero maple syrup, rice vinegar, sesame oil, garlic, and ginger.
3. In another bowl, mix the xanthan gum with water to create a slurry.
4. Add the slurry to the teriyaki sauce and mix well.
5. Place the shrimps in a bowl and season with black pepper and salt.
6. Pour the teriyaki sauce over the shrimp and mix until well-coated.
7. Place the seasoned shrimp in the air fryer basket in a single layer.
8. Air fry for 5-6 minutes until the shrimp are pink and cooked well.
9. Garnish the shrimp with sesame seeds and sliced green onions.
10. Enjoy your low-carb air fryer teriyaki shrimp!

Nutritional Information (140g per serving):
Calories: 158| Fat: 4 g| Sodium: 1076 mg| Carbs: 9 g| Fiber: 0 g| Sugars: 7 g| Protein: 22 g

Spinach Stuffed Salmon

Prep time: 15 minutes. | **Cook time:** 10 minutes.
Serves: 4

Ingredients:

- 4 salmon fillets (6 ounces each)
- 2 cups fresh spinach
- ½ cup cream cheese
- ¼ cup grated Parmesan cheese
- 1 teaspoon minced garlic
- ¼ teaspoon salt
- ¼ teaspoon black pepper
- 2 tablespoons olive oil

Directions:

1. At 375°F, preheat your air fryer.
2. In a suitable mixing bowl, combine the spinach, cream cheese, Parmesan cheese, garlic, black pepper and salt.
3. Place the salmon fillets with their skin side down on a cutting board.
4. With a sharp knife, cut a deep slit along the length of each fillet without cutting all the way through.
5. Stuff the spinach mixture into the slit of each fillet.
6. Brush the tops of the salmon fillets with olive oil.
7. Place the stuffed salmon fillets in the air fryer basket, skin side down.
8. Air fry for 10 minutes until the salmon is tender.
9. Serve immediately and enjoy your air fryer spinach stuffed salmon!

Nutritional Information (190g per serving):
Calories: 540| Fat: 41 g| Sodium: 559 mg| Carbs: 4 g| Fiber: 1 g| Sugars: 1 g| Protein: 39 g

Parmesan Calamari

Prep time: 10 minutes. | **Cook time:** 6 minutes.
Serves: 4

Ingredients:

- 1 pound calamari rings
- ½ cup almond flour
- ¼ cup grated Parmesan cheese
- 1 teaspoon paprika
- ½ teaspoon garlic powder
- ¼ teaspoon salt
- ¼ teaspoon black pepper
- 2 eggs, beaten
- Olive oil or cooking spray

Directions:

1. At 400°F, preheat your air fryer.
2. In a suitable mixing bowl, mix the almond flour, Parmesan cheese, paprika, garlic powder, black pepper and salt.
3. Dip the calamari rings in the beaten eggs and then coat the rings with the almond flour mixture.
4. Place the coated calamari rings in one single layer in the air fryer basket.
5. Spray the calamari rings with olive oil or cooking spray.
6. Air fry for 5-6 minutes until the calamari is crispy and golden brown.
7. Serve immediately with your favorite low-carb dipping sauce, such as lemon garlic aioli or sugar-free marinara sauce and enjoy.

Nutritional Information (130g per serving):
Calories: 317| Fat: 16 g| Sodium: 682 mg| Carbs: 10 g| Fiber: 3 g| Sugars: 1 g| Protein: 34 g

Crusted Cod

Prep time: 10 minutes. | **Cook time:** 10 minutes.
Serves: 4

Ingredients:

- 4 cod fillets (6 ounces each)
- ½ cup almond flour
- ¼ cup grated parmesan cheese
- 1 teaspoon garlic powder
- 1 teaspoon smoked paprika
- Salt and black pepper, to taste
- 2 eggs, beaten
- Cooking spray

Directions:

1. At 390°F, preheat your air fryer.
2. In a shallow glass bowl, mix almond flour, parmesan cheese, garlic powder, smoked paprika, black pepper and salt.
3. Dip the cod fillets into the beaten eggs, then coat the fillets with the almond flour mixture.
4. Use a spritz of cooking spray to lightly grease your air fryer basket.
5. Place the coated cod fillets into the air fryer basket without overlapping.
6. Air fry the cod fillets for 10 minutes until golden brown.
7. Serve the air fryer-crusted cod with your favorite dipping sauce.
8. Enjoy with sauteed vegetables on the side.

Nutritional Information (190g per serving):
Calories: 338| Fat: 17 g| Sodium: 561 mg| Carbs: 5 g| Fiber: 2 g| Sugars: 0 g| Protein: 39 g

Crusted Scallops

Prep time: 10 minutes. | **Cook time:** 8 minutes.
Serves: 4

Ingredients:

- 1 pound fresh sea scallops
- 1 tablespoon olive oil
- ½ teaspoon garlic powder
- ½ teaspoon paprika
- ½ teaspoon salt
- ¼ teaspoon black pepper
- ¼ cup almond flour

Directions:

1. At 400°F, preheat your air fryer.
2. Rinse and pat dry the scallops. Remove the tough muscle on the side of each scallop if needed.
3. In a shallow glass bowl, mix the olive oil, garlic powder, paprika, black pepper and salt.

4. Add the scallops to the bowl and toss to coat them well with the seasoning mixture.
5. In a separate shallow bowl, spread the almond flour.
6. Take each scallop and dip it into the almond flour, pressing it gently to coat it evenly.
7. Spread the scallops into the air fryer basket without overlapping.
8. Air fry the scallops for 6-8 minutes until they are golden brown.
9. Serve the low-carb air fryer scallops hot with lemon wedges or your favorite dipping sauce and enjoy.

Nutritional Information (100g per serving):
Calories: 176| Fat: 7 g| Sodium: 418 mg| Carbs: 5 g| Fiber: 2 g| Sugars: 0 g| Protein: 22 g

Fish Schnitzel

Prep time: 10 minutes. | **Cook time**: 10 minutes.
Serves: 4

Ingredients:

- 4 tilapia fish fillets (6 ounces each)
- ½ cup almond flour
- ¼ cup grated parmesan cheese
- 1 teaspoon garlic powder
- 1 teaspoon smoked paprika
- Salt and black pepper, to taste
- 2 eggs, beaten
- Cooking spray

Directions:

1. At 390°F, preheat your air fryer.
2. In a shallow glass bowl, mix the almond flour, parmesan cheese, garlic powder, smoked paprika, black pepper and salt.
3. Dip the fish fillets into the beaten eggs, then coat the fillets with the almond flour mixture.
4. Use a spritz of cooking spray to lightly grease your air fryer basket.
5. Place the coated fish fillets into the air fryer basket without overlapping.
6. Air fry the fish fillets for 10 minutes until golden brown.
7. Serve the air fryer fish schnitzel with your favorite dipping sauce, and enjoy!

Nutritional Information (200g per serving):
Calories: 332| Fat: 17 g| Sodium: 561 mg| Carbs: 5 g| Fiber: 2 g| Sugars: 0 g| Protein: 38 g

Shrimp Fajita

Prep time: 10 minutes. | **Cook time**: 10 minutes.
Serves: 4

Ingredients:

- 1 pound raw shrimp, peeled and deveined
- 3 bell peppers (red, green, and yellow) sliced into thin strips
- 1 large onion, sliced into thin strips
- 2 tablespoons olive oil
- 2 teaspoons chili powder
- 1 teaspoon ground cumin
- ½ teaspoon garlic powder
- ½ teaspoon smoked paprika
- Salt and black pepper, to taste
- Juice of 1 lime
- Fresh cilantro and chopped
- tortillas for serving (optional)

Directions:

1. At 400°F, preheat your air fryer.
2. In a suitable bowl, combine the shrimp, bell peppers, and onion.
3. In a suitable glass bowl, mix the olive oil, chili powder, ground cumin, garlic powder, smoked paprika, black pepper and salt.
4. Pour the spice mixture over the shrimp and vegetables and toss to coat them evenly.
5. Use a spritz of cooking spray to lightly grease your air fryer basket.
6. Add the shrimp and vegetables to the air fryer basket and air fry for 10 minutes, stirring halfway through, until the shrimp are pink and cooked well and the vegetables are tender.
7. Pour lime juice over the shrimp and vegetables and sprinkle with chopped cilantro.

8. Serve the air fryer shrimp fajita mixture with tortillas or over a bed of lettuce or cauliflower rice, if desired.
9. Enjoy with sauteed vegetables on the side.

Nutritional Information (170g per serving):
Calories: 243| Fat: 9 g| Sodium: 487 mg| Carbs: 15 g| Fiber: 4 g| Sugars: 7 g| Protein: 25 g

Fish Tacos

Prep time: 20 minutes. | **Cook time**: 10 minutes. Serves: 2

Ingredients:

- 1 pound white fish (cod or tilapia), cut into 1-inch pieces
- ¼ cup almond flour
- ¼ cup coconut flour
- 1 teaspoon garlic powder
- 1 teaspoon chili powder
- ½ teaspoon smoked paprika
- Salt and black pepper, to taste
- 2 eggs, beaten

Tacos:

- 2 tortillas
- ¼ cup shredded lettuce
- ¼ cup diced tomatoes
- ¼ cup sliced avocado
- ¼ cup sliced jalapeños
- 2 tablespoons fresh cilantro
- 4 Lime wedges
- Cooking spray

Directions:

1. At 400°F, preheat your air fryer.
2. In a shallow glass bowl, mix the almond flour, coconut flour, garlic powder, chili powder, smoked paprika, black pepper and salt.
3. Dip each piece of fish into the beaten eggs, then coat it in the flour mixture, shaking off any excess.
4. Use a spritz of cooking spray to lightly grease your air fryer basket.
5. Place the coated fish pieces in the air fryer basket, making sure they are not too crowded.
6. Air fry the coated fish for 10 minutes, flip halfway through.
7. To assemble the tacos, warm up the tortillas and fill them with shredded lettuce, diced tomatoes, sliced avocado, sliced jalapeños, and fresh cilantro.
8. Top each taco with a few pieces of air-fried fish and a squeeze of lime juice.
9. Enjoy with your favorite dipping sauce.

Nutritional Information (230g per serving):
Calories: 521| Fat: 27g| Sodium: 584mg| Carbs: 32g| Fiber: 12g| Sugars: 5g| Protein: 41g

Bacon Wrapped Shrimp

Prep time: 15 minutes. | **Cook time:** 10 minutes. | Serves: 6

Ingredients:

- 12 large shrimp, peeled and deveined
- 6 slices of sugar-free bacon
- 1 teaspoon garlic powder
- 1 teaspoon paprika
- Black pepper and salt, to taste
- Wooden skewers

Directions:

1. At 375 °F, preheat your air fryer.
2. Cut each slice of bacon in half.
3. In a suitable bowl, mix the garlic powder, paprika, black pepper and salt.
4. Season each shrimp with the spice mixture.
5. Wrap each shrimp with a half slice of bacon and secure with a wooden skewer.
6. Place the bacon-wrapped shrimp in one single layer in the air fryer basket.
7. Cook the shrimp for 10 minutes until the bacon is crispy.
8. Serve immediately with your favorite dipping sauce.
9. Enjoy your delicious and crispy bacon-wrapped shrimp straight from the air fryer!

Nutritional Information (150g per serving):
Calories: 131| Fat: 8g| Sodium: 360mg| Carbs: 0.6g| Fiber: 0.1g| Sugars: 0g| Protein: 14g

Bacon Wrapped Scallop

Prep time: 10 minutes. | **Cook time:** 10 minutes. | **Serves:** 6

Ingredients:

- 12 large sea scallops
- 6 slices of sugar-free bacon
- 1 teaspoon garlic powder
- 1 teaspoon paprika
- Black pepper and salt, to taste
- Wooden skewers

Directions:

1. At 375 °F, preheat your air fryer.
2. Cut each slice of bacon in half.
3. In a suitable bowl, mix the garlic powder, paprika, black pepper and salt.
4. Season each scallop with the spice mixture.
5. Wrap each scallop with a half slice of bacon and secure with a wooden skewer.
6. Place the bacon-wrapped scallops in one single layer in the air fryer basket.
7. Cook the scallops for 10 minutes until the bacon is crispy.
8. Serve immediately with your favorite dipping sauce.
9. Enjoy with your favorite dipping sauce.

Nutritional Information (130g per serving):
Calories: 311|Fat: 20g| Sodium: 877mg|Carbs: 3g|Fiber: 0g|Sugar: 0g| Protein: 27g

Shrimp Kung Pao

Prep time: 15 minutes. | **Cook time:** 7 minutes. | **Serves:** 4

Ingredients:

- 1 lb large shrimp, peeled and deveined
- ¼ cup low-Sodium: soy sauce
- 2 tablespoons rice vinegar
- 2 tablespoons Swerve
- 1 tablespoon sesame oil
- 1 tablespoon grated ginger
- 2 garlic cloves, minced
- 2 tablespoons chopped green onions
- 1 tablespoon crushed red pepper flakes
- ½ cup chopped peanuts
- Black pepper and salt, to taste

Directions:

1. At 400 °F, preheat your air fryer.
2. In a suitable bowl, mix well the soy sauce, rice vinegar, Swerve, sesame oil, ginger, garlic, green onions, and red pepper flakes.
3. Season the shrimp with black pepper and salt, and toss them in the sauce to coat.
4. Arrange the seasoned shrimp in one single layer in the air fryer basket.
5. Cook the shrimp for 7 minutes, shaking the basket once cooked halfway through, until the shrimp are cooked well and slightly crispy.
6. Toss them with the chopped peanuts.
7. Serve immediately and enjoy your delicious and low-carb shrimp kung pao!

Nutritional Information (130g per serving):
Calories: 221|Fat: 12.8 g| Sodium: 624 mg|Carbs: 7.3 g|Fiber: 2.3 g| Sugars: 1.3 g| Protein: 20.6 g

Fish Sticks

Prep time: 10 minutes. | **Cook time:** 10 minutes. | **Serves:** 2

Ingredients:

- 1 lb white fish fillets, cod or tilapia
- ½ cup almond flour
- ¼ cup grated parmesan cheese
- 1 teaspoon garlic powder
- 1 teaspoon dried parsley
- ½ teaspoon salt
- ¼ teaspoon black pepper
- 2 large eggs
- Cooking spray

Directions:

1. At 400 °F, preheat your air fryer.

2. Cut the fillets into strips, roughly 1 inch wide.
3. In a shallow dish, mix the almond flour, parmesan cheese, garlic powder, dried parsley, black pepper and salt.
4. In another shallow dish, whisk the eggs until lightly beaten.
5. Dip each fish strip first into the egg mixture, then into the almond flour mixture, shaking off any excess.
6. Place the coated fish strips on a suitable plate.
7. Use a spritz of cooking spray to lightly grease your air fryer basket.
8. Arrange the fish strips in one single layer in the air fryer basket, without overlapping.
9. Spray the tops of the fish strips with cooking spray.
10. Cook the fish strips for 10 minutes, flip them halfway through, until they are golden brown and crispy.
11. Serve immediately with your favorite dipping sauce.

Nutritional Information (170g per serving):
Calories: 460|Fat: 24g|Carbs: 13g|Fiber: 6g|Sugar: 1g| Protein: 47g

Fried Mahi-Mahi

Prep time: 15 minutes. | **Cook time:** 10 minutes. | Serves: 4

Ingredients:

- 4 mahi-mahi fillets
- 2 tablespoons olive oil
- 1 tablespoon lemon juice
- 1 teaspoon paprika
- ½ teaspoon garlic powder
- ½ teaspoon dried thyme
- Black pepper and salt, to taste

Directions:

1. At 375 °F, preheat your air fryer.
2. In a suitable bowl, mix the olive oil, lemon juice, paprika, garlic powder, dried thyme, black pepper and salt.
3. Brush the mixture on both sides of the mahi-mahi fillets.
4. Place the fillets in one single layer in the air fryer basket.
5. Cook the fillets for 10 minutes, flip them halfway through, until they are golden brown and cooked through.
6. Serve immediately with your favorite side dish.
7. Enjoy your delicious and easy air fryer mahi-mahi!

Nutritional Information (170g per serving):
Calories: 212| Fat: 11 g| Sodium: 289 mg| Carbs: 2 g| Fiber: 1 g| Sugars: 0 g| Protein: 27 g

Maple Glazed Tuna Steaks

Prep time: 10 minutes. | **Cook time:** 7 minutes. | Serves: 2

Ingredients:

- 2 tuna steak (6 ounces each)
- 1 tablespoon olive oil
- 1 teaspoon soy sauce
- 1 teaspoon sesame oil
- 1 teaspoon ChocZero maple syrup
- 1 teaspoon grated ginger
- 1 garlic clove, minced
- Black pepper and salt, to taste

Directions:

1. At 400 °F, preheat your air fryer.
2. In a suitable bowl, mix the olive oil, soy sauce, sesame oil, ChocZero maple syrup, grated ginger, minced garlic, black pepper and salt.
3. Rub the prepared spice mixture on both sides of the tuna steaks.
4. Place the tuna steaks in one single layer in the air fryer basket.
5. Cook the tuna steaks for 7 minutes, flip them halfway through, until they are cooked well but still slightly pink in the center.
6. Enjoy your delicious and healthy air fryer tuna steaks!

Nutritional Information (170g per serving):
Calories: 350| Fat: 16g| Sodium: 340mg| Carbs: 8g| Fiber: 0g| Sugars: 7g| Protein: 40g

Crispy Oysters

Prep time: 15 minutes. | **Cook time:** 10 minutes. | **Serves:** 6

Ingredients:

- 12 fresh oysters (2 ounces each), shucked
- ¼ cup almond flour
- ¼ cup grated Parmesan cheese
- 1 teaspoon garlic powder
- ½ teaspoon paprika
- Black pepper and salt, to taste
- Cooking spray

Directions:

1. At 375 °F, preheat your air fryer.
2. In a suitable bowl, mix the almond flour, Parmesan cheese, garlic powder, paprika, black pepper and salt.
3. Dip each oyster in the mixture, pressing the coating onto the oyster to make it stick.
4. Use a spritz of cooking spray to lightly grease your air fryer basket.
5. Arrange the oysters in one single layer in the air fryer basket, without overlapping.
6. Spray the tops of the oysters with cooking spray.
7. Cook the oysters for 10 minutes, until they are golden brown and crispy.
8. Serve right away with wedges of lemon and your favorite dipping sauce.
9. Enjoy your delicious and low-carb air fryer oysters!

Nutritional Information (100g per serving):
Calories: 164|Fat: 10g| Sodium: 220mg |Carbs: 5g|Fiber: 2g|Sugars: 3g| Protein: 12g

Crusted Haddock

Prep time: 15 minutes. | **Cook time:** 10 minutes. | **Serves:** 4

Ingredients:

- 4 haddock fillets (6 ounces each)
- ¼ cup almond flour
- ¼ cup grated parmesan cheese
- 1 teaspoon garlic powder
- ½ teaspoon paprika
- Black pepper and salt, to taste
- Cooking spray

Directions:

1. At 400 °F, preheat your air fryer.
2. In a suitable bowl, mix the almond flour, parmesan cheese, garlic powder, paprika, black pepper and salt.
3. Dip each haddock fillet in the mixture, pressing the coating onto the fish to make it stick.
4. Use a spritz of cooking spray to lightly grease your air fryer basket.
5. Arrange the haddock fillets in one single layer in the air fryer basket.
6. Spray the tops of the haddock fillets with cooking spray.
7. Cook the haddock fillets for 10 minutes, flip them halfway through, until golden brown.
8. Serve immediately with lemon wedges and your favorite side dish.
9. Enjoy your delicious and healthy air fryer haddock!

Nutritional Information (180g per serving):
Calories: 218|Fat: 11.7 g| Sodium: 300mg |Carbs: 12g | Fiber: 1.3 g| Sugars: 1.9 g| Protein: 23.6 g

Crab Rangoon

Prep time: 10 minutes. | **Cook time:** 10 minutes. | **Serves:** 4

Ingredients:

- 4 ounces lump crab meat, drained
- 4 ounces cream cheese, softened
- 2 green onions, chopped
- 1 clove garlic, minced
- 1 teaspoon Worcestershire sauce
- Black pepper and salt, to taste
- 12 wonton wrappers
- Cooking spray

Directions:

1. At 375 °F, preheat your air fryer.
2. In a suitable bowl, mix the crab meat, cream cheese, green onions, garlic, Worcestershire sauce, black pepper and salt.
3. On a flat surface, spread the wonton wrappers out.
4. Place a teaspoon of the crab mixture in the center of each wrapper.
5. Wet the edges of these wrappers with a little bit of water, then fold the wrapper in half to form a triangle.
6. To seal the wrapper, simply press the edges together.
7. Use a spritz of cooking spray to lightly grease your air fryer basket.
8. Place the crab Rangoon in one single layer in the air fryer basket.
9. Spray the tops of the crab Rangoon with cooking spray.
10. Cook the crab Rangoon for 10 minutes, until they are golden brown and crispy.
11. Serve and enjoy with your favorite dipping sauce.

Nutritional Information (150g per serving):
Calories: 316|Fat: 15g| Sodium: 310mg |Carbs: 27g|Fiber: 1g|Sugar: 1g| Protein: 17g

Crab Stuffed Mushrooms

Prep time: 15 minutes. | **Cook time:** 10 minutes. | **Serves:** 12

Ingredients:

- 12 large mushrooms
- 4 ounces lump crab meat, drained
- 2 ounces cream cheese, softened
- 2 tablespoons grated parmesan cheese
- 1 green onion, chopped
- 1 clove garlic, minced
- Black pepper and salt, to taste
- Cooking spray

Directions:

1. At 375 °F, preheat your air fryer.
2. Clean the mushrooms and remove the stems.
3. In a suitable bowl, mix the crab meat, cream cheese, parmesan cheese, green onion, garlic, black pepper and salt.
4. Stuff each mushroom cap with the crab mixture, making sure to pack it tightly.
5. Use a spritz of cooking spray to lightly grease your air fryer basket.
6. Place the stuffed mushrooms in one single layer in the air fryer basket.
7. Spray the tops of the stuffed mushrooms with cooking spray.
8. Cook the stuffed mushrooms for 10 minutes, until they are golden.
9. Serve immediately with your favorite dipping sauce.
10. Enjoy your delicious and low-carb air fryer crab stuffed mushrooms.

Nutritional Information (150g per serving):
Calories: 103|Fat: 6.6 g| Sodium: 411mg |Carbs: 3.3 g|Fiber: 0.7 g|Sugar: 1.2 g| Protein: 7.7 g

Tuna Patties

Prep time: 10 minutes. | **Cook time:** 10 minutes. | **Serves:** 2

Ingredients:

- 2 cans of tuna, drained
- 2 eggs
- ¼ cup almond flour
- 2 tablespoons chopped parsley
- ½ teaspoon garlic powder
- Black pepper and salt, to taste
- Cooking spray

Directions:

1. At 400 °F, preheat your air fryer.
2. In a suitable bowl, mix the tuna, eggs, almond flour, parsley, garlic powder, black pepper and salt.
3. Form the mixture into 6-8 patties.
4. Use a spritz of cooking spray to lightly grease your air fryer basket.
5. Place the tuna patties in one single layer in the air fryer basket.
6. Spray the tops of the tuna patties with cooking spray.
7. Cook the tuna patties for 10 minutes, flip them halfway through.
8. Serve immediately with your favorite side dish.

Nutritional Information (140g per serving):
Calories: 332| Fat: 19g| Sodium: 606mg| Carbs: 4.4g| Fiber: 1.7g| Sugars: 0.5g| Protein: 38g

Blackened Salmon

Prep time: 15 minutes. | **Cook time:** 10 minutes. | **Serves:** 2

Ingredients:

- 2 salmon fillets (6 ounces each), skin-on
- 1 tablespoon smoked paprika
- 1 teaspoon garlic powder
- 1 teaspoon onion powder
- 1 teaspoon dried thyme
- 1 teaspoon dried oregano
- 1 teaspoon salt
- ½ teaspoon black pepper
- Cooking spray

Directions:

1. At 400 °F, preheat your air fryer.
2. In a suitable bowl, mix the smoked paprika, garlic and onion powder, dried thyme, dried oregano, black pepper and salt.
3. Pat the salmon fillets dry with a paper towel and keep them skin-side down on a suitable plate.
4. Rub the spice mixture all over the flesh side of the salmon fillets, making sure to coat them evenly.
5. Use a spritz of cooking spray to lightly grease your air fryer basket.
6. Place the salmon fillets in one single layer in the air fryer basket, skin-side down.
7. Spray the tops of the salmon fillets with cooking spray.
8. Cook the salmon fillets for 10 minutes, until they are cooked well and blackened on the outside.
9. Remove the salmon fillets from the air fryer and let them cool for a 5-10 minutes.
10. Serve immediately with your favorite side dish.

Nutritional Information (170g per serving):
Calories: 332| Fat: 19g| Sodium: 601mg| Carbs: 4.4g| Fiber: 1.7g| Sugars: 0.5g| Protein: 38g

Chapter 7: Pork, Beef and Lamb

Meatball Subs

Prep time: 10 minutes. | **Cook time:** 19 minutes. | **Serves:** 6

Ingredients:

- 1 pound 85% lean ground beef
- ½ cup Italian bread crumbs
- 1 (18-ounce) jar marinara sauce
- 1½ cups shredded mozzarella cheese
- 1 tablespoon dried minced onion
- 1 tablespoon minced garlic
- 1 large egg
- 1 teaspoon salt
- 1 teaspoon black pepper
- 6 hoagie rolls
- Cooking spray

Directions:

1. At 350°F, preheat your air fryer.
2. Line your air fryer basket with parchment and spray lightly with oil.
3. In a bowl, mix the beef, bread crumbs, onion, garlic, egg, black pepper and salt. Roll the mixture into 18 meatballs.
4. Place the meatballs in the prepared basket. When the Unit is preheated, slide the basket into the air fryer and begin cooking for 15 minutes until done.
5. Place 3 meatballs in each hoagie roll. Top with marinara and mozzarella cheese. Place the loaded rolls in the air fryer and air fry for 3 to 4 minutes, until the cheese is melted. Serve immediately.

Nutritional Information (156g per serving):
Calories 338| Fat: 10.8g | Sodium: 870mg | Carbs:24g | Fiber 2g | Sugar: 3g| Protein: 34g

Garlicky Buttery Steak Bites

Prep time: 15 minutes. | **Cook time:** 16 minutes. | **Serves:** 3

Ingredients:

- 1 pound boneless steak, cut into 1-inch pieces
- 2 tablespoons olive oil
- 1 teaspoon Worcestershire sauce
- ½ teaspoon granulated garlic
- ½ teaspoon salt
- ¼ teaspoon black pepper
- Cooking spray

Directions:

1. At 400°F, preheat your air fryer.
2. Line your air fryer basket with parchment and spray lightly with oil.
3. In a bowl, combine the steak, olive oil, Worcestershire sauce, garlic, black pepper and salt and toss until evenly coated.
4. Place this steak in one single layer in the prepared basket.
5. When the Unit is preheated, slide the basket into the air fryer and begin cooking for 16 minutes, flip every 3 to 4 minutes. Serve hot.

Nutritional Information (164g per serving):
Calories 387| Fat: 24.3g | Sodium: 724mg | Carbs:1g | Fiber 0g | Sugar: 0g| Protein: 42g

Steak Tips with Roasted Potatoes

Prep time: 10 minutes. | **Cook time:** 24 minutes. | **Serves:** 2

Ingredients:

- 1 pound steak, cut into ½-inch pieces
- 8 ounces baby gold potatoes, cut in half
- ½ teaspoon salt
- 1 teaspoon Worcestershire sauce
- 1 teaspoon granulated garlic
- ½ teaspoon salt
- ½ teaspoon black pepper
- Cooking spray

Directions:

1. At 400°F, preheat your air fryer.
2. Line your air fryer basket with parchment and spray lightly with oil.
3. In a microwave-safe bowl, combine the potatoes and salt, then pour in about ½ inch of water. Microwave for 7 minutes until the potatoes are nearly tender. Drain.
4. In a bowl, gently mix the steak, potatoes, Worcestershire sauce, garlic, black pepper and salt. Spread the prepared mixture in an even layer in the prepared basket.
5. When the Unit is preheated, slide the basket into the air fryer and begin cooking for 17 minutes until done.
6. Enjoy the steak with potatoes.

Nutritional Information (210g per serving):
Calories 375| Fat: 14.6g | Sodium: 861mg | Carbs:15g | Fiber 1g | Sugar: 1g| Protein: 43g

Bacon Wrapped Filet Mignon

Prep time: 15 minutes. | **Cook time:** 15 minutes. | **Serves:** 2

Ingredients:

- 2 filet mignon steaks (6 ounces)
- 2 slices of sugar-free bacon
- 2 toothpicks
- 1 teaspoon cracked peppercorns
- 1/2 teaspoon kosher salt
- Avocado oil

Directions:

1. To prepare the bacon-wrapped filet mignon, take a slice of bacon and wrap it around the filet mignon.
2. Use a toothpick to secure the bacon in place by piercing it through the bacon and into the filet, then out of the filet and into the bacon on the other side of the toothpick.
3. Next, season the steak with salt, pepper, or your preferred seasonings.
4. Place the bacon-wrapped filet mignon on the rack of your air fryer and spray a bit of avocado oil onto the steak.
5. Set the temperature to 375 degrees F and air fry the steak for about 10 minutes.
6. Then, flip the steak to cook the other side for another 5 minutes, or until it reaches the desired level of doneness.
7. Serve warm with your favorite salad.

Nutritional Information (180g per serving):
Calories 557| Fat: 26.9g | Sodium: 129mg | Carbs:2g | Fiber 0g | Sugar: 0g| Protein: 29g

Mongolian Beef

Prep time: 10 minutes. | **Cook time:** 10 minutes. | **Serves:** 4

Ingredients:

- 1 pound flank steak, thinly sliced
- ¼ cup xanthan gum
- ¾ cup packed light Swerve
- ½ cup soy sauce
- 2 teaspoons toasted sesame oil
- 1 tablespoon minced garlic
- ½ teaspoon ground ginger
- ½ cup water
- ½ cup cooked brown rice, for serving(Optional)
- Cooking spray

Directions:

1. At 360°F, preheat your air fryer.
2. Line your air fryer basket with parchment and spray lightly with oil.

3. Place the xanthan gum in a bowl and dredge the steak until evenly coated. Shake off any excess xanthan gum.
4. Place this steak in the prepared basket and spray lightly with oil.
5. When the Unit is preheated, slide the basket in the air fryer and begin cooking for 5 minutes, flip, and air fry for another 5 minutes.
6. In a suitable saucepan, combine the Swerve, soy sauce, sesame oil, garlic, ginger, and water and cook to a boil over medium-high heat, stirring frequently.
7. Remove from the heat. Transfer the meat to the sauce and toss until evenly coated. Let sit for about 5 minutes so the steak absorbs the flavors.
8. Serve with white rice or ramen noodles.
9. Enjoy warm with sauteed vegetables.

Nutritional Information (204g per serving):
Calories 324| Fat: 14.7g | Sodium: 556mg | Carbs:19g | Fiber 1g | Sugar: 7g| Protein: 27g

Pepperoni Pizza

Prep time: 10 minutes. | **Cook time:** 55 minutes. | Serves: 6

Ingredients:

- 1 cup shredded mozzarella cheese
- 1/4 cup almond flour
- 1 egg
- 1/4 teaspoon salt
- 1/4 teaspoon garlic powder
- 1/4 teaspoon dried oregano
- 1/4 cup low-carb pizza sauce
- 1/4 cup shredded Parmesan cheese
- 1/4 cup sliced pepperoni

Directions:

1. First, combine shredded mozzarella cheese, almond flour, egg, salt, garlic powder, and dried oregano in a mixing bowl, and mix thoroughly to form a dough.
2. Divide this pizza dough into two equal portions and shape them into balls.
3. Flatten each dough ball into a circle using your hands and place them on separate pieces of parchment paper.
4. At 375°F, preheat your air fryer.
5. Transfer the parchment paper with the pizza dough onto the air fryer basket and cook for 5 minutes.
6. Remove the pizza crust from the air fryer basket, leaving it on the parchment paper.
7. Spread low-carb pizza sauce over the crust, leaving a small border around the edges, then sprinkle with Parmesan cheese and sliced pepperoni.
8. Return the pizza to the air fryer and cook for an additional 5-7 minutes, or until the cheese has melted and is bubbly.
9. Finally, use a spatula to remove the pizza from the air fryer basket and transfer it to a cutting board.
10. Slice and serve immediately.

Nutritional Information (156g per serving):
Calories 434| Fat: 36.4g | Sodium: 998mg | Carbs:2.6g | Fiber 0.8g | Sugar: 0.8g| Protein: 24g

Cheese Stuffed Kebabs

Prep time: 20 minutes. | **Cook time:** 15 minutes. | Serves: 4

Ingredients:

- 1 lb ground beef
- ½ cup shredded cheese
- 1 bell pepper, chopped into bite-sized pieces
- 1 onion, chopped into bite-sized pieces
- 1 teaspoon garlic powder
- 1 teaspoon onion powder
- 1 teaspoon dried oregano
- ½ teaspoon salt
- ¼ teaspoon black pepper
- 8 skewers
- Cooking spray

Directions:

1. At 400 °F, preheat your air fryer.

2. In a suitable bowl, mix the ground beef, garlic and onion powder, oregano, black pepper and salt until well combined.
3. Divide the meat mixture into 8 equal portions.
4. Flatten each portion into a thin patty.
5. Place a spoonful of shredded cheese in the center of each patty.
6. Roll the patty around the cheese to form a ball.
7. Thread the meatballs onto skewers, alternating with pieces of bell pepper and onion.
8. Lightly spray the skewers with cooking spray.
9. Place the skewers in the air fryer basket.
10. Air fry for 15 minutes, until the meatballs are cooked well and the vegetables are tender.
11. Carefully remove the skewers from the air fryer basket, and serve hot.
12. Enjoy with sauteed vegetables.

Nutritional Information (170g per serving):
Calories: 485| Fat: 33g| Sodium: 570mg| Carbs: 9g| Fiber: 2g| Sugars: 4g| Protein: 36g

Stuffed Bell Pepper

Prep time: 15 minutes. | **Cook time:** 20 minutes. | Serves: 4

Ingredients:

- 16 ounces ground beef
- 4 bell peppers, cut top of bell pepper
- 2/3 cup cheese, shredded
- ½ cup rice, cooked
- 1 teaspoon basil, dried
- ½ teaspoon chili powder
- 1 teaspoon black pepper
- 1 teaspoon garlic salt
- 2 teaspoon Worcestershire sauce
- 8 ounces tomato sauce
- 2 garlic cloves, minced
- 1 small onion, chopped
- Cooking spray, for spraying

Directions:

1. At 400 °F, preheat your air fryer.
2. Grease a frying pan with cooking oil and fry the onion and garlic over medium heat.
3. Stir in the beef, basil, chili powder, black pepper, and garlic salt, combining everything well.
4. Allow cooking until the beef is nicely browned before taking the pan off the heat. Add in half of the cheese, the rice, Worcestershire sauce, and tomato sauce and stir to combine. Spoon equal amounts of the beef mixture into the four bell peppers, filling them entirely.
5. Grease the basket with cooking spray. Put the stuffed bell peppers in the basket and allow to air fry for 11 minutes.
6. Add the cheese on top of bell pepper with the remaining cheese and air fry for a further 2 minutes.
7. When the cheese is melted and the bell peppers are piping hot, serve immediately.
8. Enjoy with your favorite salad on the side.

Nutritional Information (294g per serving):
Calories 584| Fat: 46g | Sodium: 795mg | Carbs:20g | Fiber 5g | Sugar: 7g| Protein: 27g

Sweet Sticky Pork Chops

Prep time: 15 minutes. | **Cook time:** 15 minutes. | Serves: 4

Ingredients:

- 4 (6-ounce) boneless pork chops
- 1 teaspoon salt
- ½ teaspoon black pepper
- ¼ cup ChocZero maple syrup
- 2 tablespoons minced garlic
- 2 tablespoons lemon juice
- 1 tablespoon sweet chili sauce
- Cooking spray

Directions:

1. At 360°F, preheat your air fryer.
2. Line your air fryer basket with parchment and spray lightly with oil.
3. Rub the black pepper and salt on both sides of the pork chops.

4. Place the chops in one single layer in the prepared basket.
5. When Unit is preheated, slide basket in the air fryer and begin cooking for 8 minutes, flip, and air fry for 7 minutes.
6. In a suitable saucepan, combine the ChocZero maple syrup, garlic, lemon juice, and sweet chili sauce and cook on a simmer over low heat.
7. Cook for 3 to 4 minutes until the sauce thickens.
8. Transfer the chops to a serving platter and pour the sauce over the top.
9. Enjoy with low-carb tortillas or sauteed vegetables.

Nutritional Information (224g per serving):
Calories 312| Fat: 6.4g | Sodium: 731mg | Carbs:20g | Fiber 0g | Sugar: 8g| Protein: 42g

Pork Schnitzel

Prep time: 10 minutes. | **Cook time:** 14 minutes. | **Serves:** 4

Ingredients:
- 4 boneless pork chops (6 ounces each), pounded to ⅓ inch thick
- ⅔ cup panko bread crumbs
- ¼ teaspoon granulated garlic
- ¼ teaspoon dried thyme
- ¼ teaspoon dried sage
- ¼ teaspoon dried rosemary
- ¼ teaspoon salt
- ¼ teaspoon black pepper
- ½ cup oat flour
- 1 large egg
- Cooking spray

Directions:
1. At 360°F preheat your air fryer.
2. Line your air fryer basket with parchment and spray lightly with oil.
3. In a bowl, mix the bread crumbs, garlic, thyme, sage, rosemary, black pepper and salt.
4. Spread the flour on a suitable plate.
5. In a bowl, whisk the egg. Dredge the chops in the oat flour, dip in the egg, and dredge in the bread crumb mixture until evenly coated.
6. Place the chops in one single layer in the prepared basket and spray with oil.
7. When Unit is preheated, slide basket in the air fryer and begin cooking for 8 minutes, flip, spray with oil, and air fry for another 5 to 6 minutes, until golden brown and the internal temperature reaches 145°F.
8. Enjoy with your favorite salad.

Nutritional Information (212g per serving):
Calories 322| Fat: 7.8g | Sodium: 267mg | Carbs:15g | Fiber 1g | Sugar: 0g| Protein: 44g

Beef Hamburgers

Prep time: 20 minutes. | **Cook time:** 27 minutes. | **Serves:** 4

Ingredients:

Buns:
- 1/2 cup almond flour
- 1/4 cup coconut flour
- 1 tsp baking powder
- 1/4 tsp salt
- 1/4 cup unsalted butter, melted
- 3 large eggs
- 2 tbsp unsweetened almond milk

Burger Patties:
- 1 lb ground beef (90% lean)
- 1/4 cup almond flour
- 1 egg
- 1/2 tsp garlic powder
- 1/2 tsp onion powder
- 1/2 tsp dried oregano
- 1/2 tsp salt
- 1/4 tsp black pepper
- 4 slices of ham
- 4 slices of cheddar cheese

Directions:

1. To start making your low-carb air fryer buns, begin by preheating your air fryer to a temperature of 350°F (175°C).
2. Next, in a mixing bowl, combine a few simple ingredients including almond flour, coconut flour, baking powder, and salt. Mix well to ensure an even blend.
3. Then, in a separate mixing bowl, whisk together melted butter, eggs, and almond milk. Once evenly combined, add the dry ingredients to the wet mixture.
4. Mix until thoroughly combined to create a smooth and creamy dough. Using a cookie scoop or spoon, divide the dough into four equal portions and shape them into round buns.
5. Carefully place the buns into the air fryer basket and cook for 10-12 minutes or until they achieve a golden brown color.
6. Keep them aside until ready to serve.
7. In a mixing bowl, combine ground beef, almond flour, egg, garlic powder, onion powder, dried oregano, salt, and black pepper.
8. Mix well until all the burger patty ingredients are well combined.
9. Divide the mixture into four equal parts and shape each part into a patty. Flatten each patty with your palm.
10. Switch the air fryer to 375°F.
11. Place the prepared hamburger patties in the air fryer basket and air fry them for 10-12 minutes, flipping once halfway through.
12. After 10-12 minutes, top each patty with a slice of ham and a slice of cheddar cheese.
13. Cook for another 3 minutes or until the cheese is melted.
14. Serve the patties in between the buns.

Nutritional Information (200g per serving):
Calories 499| Fat: 25.4g | Sodium: 921mg | Carbs:4.6g | Fiber 0.7g | Sugar: 0.4g| Protein: 48g

Mushroom Stuffed Pork

Prep time: 15 minutes. | **Cook time:** 20 minutes. | Serves: 2

Ingredients:

- 4 pork chops (6 ounces each), boneless, 1 inch thick
- ½ cup chopped onion
- ½ cup chopped mushrooms
- ½ cup chopped spinach
- ½ cup shredded mozzarella cheese
- ¼ cup grated Parmesan cheese
- 1 teaspoon dried thyme
- 1 teaspoon dried rosemary
- Black pepper and salt, to taste
- Cooking spray

Directions:

1. At 375 °F, preheat your air fryer.
2. In a suitable mixing bowl, combine the chopped onion, mushrooms, spinach, mozzarella cheese, Parmesan cheese, thyme, rosemary, black pepper and salt.
3. Use a sharp knife to create a pocket in each pork chop, making sure not to cut all the way through.
4. Stuff each pork chop with the vegetable and cheese mixture, using toothpicks to secure the opening if needed.
5. Use a spritz of cooking spray to lightly grease your air fryer basket.
6. Place the stuffed pork chops in the air fryer basket.
7. Cook in the air fry for 18-20 minutes until the pork is cooked well and the filling is hot and bubbly.
8. Remove the stuffed pork chops from the air fryer with care, and then give them some time to rest.
9. Remove the toothpicks before serving.
10. Enjoy with your favorite salad.

Nutritional Information (170g per serving):
Calories: 398| Fat: 22g| Sodium: 455mg| Carbs: 4.4g| Fiber: 1.2g| Sugars: 1.6g| Protein: 42g

Bacon Wrapped Pork Tenderloin

Prep time: 10 minutes. | **Cook time:** 25 minutes. | **Serves:** 2

Ingredients:

- 1 pork tenderloin, about 1 lb
- 8-10 slices of sugar-free bacon
- 1 teaspoon garlic powder
- 1 teaspoon smoked paprika
- Black pepper and salt, to taste
- Cooking spray

Directions:

1. At 400 °F, preheat your air fryer.
2. Season the pork tenderloin with garlic powder, smoked paprika, black pepper and salt.
3. Wrap the bacon slices around the pork tenderloin, tucking the ends underneath.
4. Use a spritz of cooking spray to lightly grease your air fryer basket.
5. Place the bacon-wrapped pork tenderloin in the air fryer basket.
6. Cook in the air fry for 25 minutes until the pork is cooked well and the bacon is crispy.
7. Slice the cooked pork tenderloin into medallions and serve.
8. Enjoy with sauteed vegetables.

Nutritional Information (170g per serving):
Calories: 517| Fat: 33g| Sodium: 791mg| Carbs: 1g| Fiber: 0g| Sugars: 0g| Protein: 51g

Roasted Pork Tenderloin

Prep time: 15 minutes. | **Cook time:** 20 minutes. | **Serves:** 2

Ingredients:

- 1 pork tenderloin, about 1 lb
- 2 teaspoons garlic powder
- 2 teaspoons onion powder
- 2 teaspoons dried thyme
- 1 teaspoon smoked paprika
- Black pepper and salt, to taste
- Cooking spray

Directions:

1. At 400 °F, preheat your air fryer.
2. Season the pork tenderloin with garlic and onion powder, dried thyme, smoked paprika, black pepper and salt.
3. Use a spritz of cooking spray to lightly grease your air fryer basket.
4. Place this pork tenderloin in the air fryer basket.
5. Cook in the air fry for 20 minutes until the pork is cooked well.
6. Slice the cooked pork tenderloin into medallions and serve.
7. Enjoy with your favorite salad.

Nutritional Information (150g per serving):
Calories: 358| Fat: 8g| Sodium: 310mg| Carbs: 6g| Fiber: 1g| Sugars: 0g| Protein: 63g

Pork Skewers

Prep time: 15 minutes. | **Cook time:** 12 minutes. | **Serves:** 2

Ingredients:

- 1 lb pork tenderloin, diced into 1-inch cubes
- 2 tablespoons olive oil
- 2 teaspoons garlic powder
- 1 teaspoon smoked paprika
- 1 teaspoon cumin
- Black pepper and salt, to taste
- Wooden or metal skewers
- Cooking spray

Directions:

1. At 400 °F, preheat your air fryer.
2. In a suitable mixing bowl, combine the pork cubes with olive oil, garlic powder, smoked paprika, cumin, black pepper and salt. Mix well to coat.
3. Thread the pork cubes onto the skewers.

4. Use a spritz of cooking spray to lightly grease your air fryer basket.
5. Place the pork skewers in the air fryer basket.
6. Cook in the air fry for 12 minutes until the pork is cooked well and the edges are slightly charred.
7. Carefully remove the pork skewers from the air fryer and serve hot.
8. Enjoy with your favorite salad.

Nutritional Information (150g per serving):
Calories: 390| Fat: 22g| Sodium: 226mg| Carbs: 3g| Fiber: 1g| Sugars: 0g| Protein: 43g

Pork Mushroom Skewer

Prep time: 10 minutes. | **Cook time:** 12 minutes. | Serves: 2

Ingredients:

- 1 lb pork tenderloin, diced into 1-inch cubes
- 8-10 large mushrooms, cleaned and stemmed
- 2 tablespoons olive oil
- 2 teaspoons garlic powder
- 1 teaspoon smoked paprika
- 1 teaspoon cumin
- Black pepper and salt, to taste
- Wooden or metal skewers
- Cooking spray

Directions:

1. At 400 °F, preheat your air fryer.
2. In a suitable mixing bowl, combine the pork cubes with olive oil, garlic powder, smoked paprika, cumin, black pepper and salt. Mix well to coat.
3. Thread the pork cubes and mushrooms onto the skewers, alternating between pork and mushrooms.
4. Use a spritz of cooking spray to lightly grease your air fryer basket.
5. Place the pork and mushroom skewers in the air fryer basket.
6. Cook in the air fry for 12 minutes until the pork is cooked well and the edges are slightly charred.
7. Carefully remove the skewers from the air fryer and serve hot.
8. Enjoy with sauteed vegetables.

Nutritional Information (170g per serving):
Calories: 374| Fat: 21g| Sodium: 56mg| Carbs: 8g| Fiber: 2g| Sugars: 4g| Protein: 43g

Chimichurri Lamb Chop

Prep time: 15 minutes. | **Cook time:** 12 minutes. | Serves: 4

Ingredients:

- 4 lamb chops (6 ounces each)
- ½ cup fresh parsley leaves, chopped
- ¼ cup fresh cilantro leaves, chopped
- 2 garlic cloves, minced
- ¼ cup olive oil
- 1 tablespoon red wine vinegar
- 1 tablespoon lemon juice
- Black pepper and salt, to taste
- Cooking spray

Directions:

1. At 400 °F, preheat your air fryer.
2. In a suitable mixing bowl, combine the parsley, cilantro, garlic, olive oil, red wine vinegar, lemon juice, black pepper and salt. Mix well to make the chimichurri sauce.
3. Season the lamb chops with black pepper and salt on both sides.
4. Use a spritz of cooking spray to lightly grease your air fryer basket.
5. Fill the air fryer basket with lamb chops.
6. Cook in the air fry for 12 minutes until the lamb is cooked.
7. Carefully remove the lamb chops from the air fryer and spoon the chimichurri sauce over the top of each chop.
8. Serve hot.

9. Enjoy with sauteed vegetables.

Nutritional Information (170g per serving):
Calories: 483| Fat: 38g| Sodium: 89mg| Carbs: 3g| Fiber: 1g| Sugars: 1g| Protein: 30g

Beef Fajita

Prep time: 15 minutes. | **Cook time:** 12 minutes. | **Serves:** 2

Ingredients:

- 1 lb beef steak, sliced into thin strips
- 1 green bell pepper, sliced
- 1 red bell pepper, sliced
- 1 yellow onion, sliced
- 2 tablespoons olive oil
- 2 teaspoons chili powder
- 1 teaspoon ground cumin
- ½ teaspoon garlic powder
- Black pepper and salt, to taste
- Optional toppings: sour cream, shredded cheese, sliced avocado, diced tomatoes, fresh cilantro

Directions:

1. At 400 °F, preheat your air fryer.
2. In a suitable mixing bowl, combine the beef strips with olive oil, chili powder, cumin, garlic powder, black pepper and salt. Mix well to coat.
3. Spread the beef strips, sliced bell peppers, and onions in one single layer in the air fryer basket.
4. Cook in the air fry for 12 minutes until the beef is cooked well.
5. Carefully remove the fajita mixture from the air fryer and serve hot with your choice of toppings.
6. Enjoy with low-carb tortillas.

Nutritional Information (160g per serving):
Calories: 443| Fat: 27g| Sodium: 163mg| Carbs: 16g| Fiber: 4g| Sugars: 8g| Protein: 34g

Lamb Kebab

Prep time: 15 minutes. | **Cook time:** 10 minutes. | **Serves:** 2

Ingredients:

- 1 lb lamb meat, cut into 1-inch cubes
- 1 red onion, cut into 1-inch chunks
- 1 green bell pepper, diced into 1-inch chunks
- 1 red bell pepper, diced into 1-inch chunks
- 2 tablespoons olive oil
- 1 teaspoon ground cumin
- 1 teaspoon paprika
- ½ teaspoon ground coriander
- ½ teaspoon garlic powder
- Black pepper and salt, to taste

Directions:

1. At 400 °F, preheat your air fryer.
2. In a suitable mixing bowl, combine the lamb cubes with olive oil, cumin, paprika, coriander, garlic powder, black pepper and salt. Mix well to coat.
3. Thread the lamb cubes, red onion chunks, and bell pepper chunks onto skewers.
4. Place the skewers in the air fryer basket in a single layer.
5. Cook in the air fry for 10 minutes until the lamb is cooked well.
6. Carefully remove the kebabs from the air fryer and serve hot.
7. Enjoy with sauteed vegetables or fresh salad.

Nutritional Information (160g per serving):
Calories: 350| Fat: 22g| Sodium: 87mg| Carbs: 10g| Fiber: 3g| Sugars: 5g| Protein: 28g

Beef Meatloaf

Prep time: 15 minutes. | **Cook time:** 35 minutes. | **Serves:** 4

Ingredients:

- 1 lb ground beef
- ½ cup almond flour
- ¼ cup grated Parmesan cheese
- ¼ cup chopped onion
- ¼ cup chopped green bell pepper
- 2 tablespoons tomato paste
- 1 tablespoon Worcestershire sauce
- 1 teaspoon garlic powder
- ½ teaspoon salt
- ¼ teaspoon black pepper
- 1 egg, beaten
- **Glaze:**
- 2 tablespoons tomato paste
- 1 tablespoon apple cider vinegar
- 1 tablespoon Swerve

Directions:

1. At 350 °F, preheat your air fryer.
2. In a suitable mixing bowl, combine the ground beef, almond flour, Parmesan cheese, onion, green bell pepper, tomato paste, Worcestershire sauce, garlic powder, salt, black pepper, and egg. Mix well to combine.
3. Form the beef mixture into a loaf shape and keep it in your air fryer basket.
4. Then air fry the meatloaf for 30 minutes.
5. In the meantime, prepare the optional glaze by combining tomato paste, apple cider vinegar, and Swerve in a suitable bowl.
6. After 30 minutes, remove the meatloaf from the air fryer and brush the prepared glaze over the top.
7. Return the cooked meatloaf to the air fryer and air fry for an additional 5-10 minutes, until the glaze is slightly caramelized and the meatloaf is cooked through.
8. Slice and serve to enjoy.
9. Enjoy with low-carb tortilla and fresh salad.

Nutritional Information (150g per serving):
Calories: 395| Fat: 27g| Sodium: 600mg| Carbs: 8g| Fiber: 3g| Sugars: 2g| Protein: 30g

Cajun Pork Chops

Prep time: 10 minutes. | **Cook time:** 12 minutes. | **Serves:** 4

Ingredients:

- 4 bone-in pork chops (6 ounces each), 1 inch thick
- 2 tablespoons olive oil
- 2 teaspoons Cajun seasoning
- ½ teaspoon garlic powder
- Black pepper and salt, to taste

Directions:

1. At 375 °F, preheat your air fryer.
2. Use some paper towels to pat dry the pork chops and brush them with olive oil.
3. Rub both sides of the pork chops liberally with Cajun seasoning, salt, garlic powder, and pepper.
4. Place the pork chops in the air fryer basket in a single layer.
5. Cook in the air fry for 12 minutes.
6. Remove the air fried pork chops from the air fryer and let them rest for 3-5 minutes before serving.
7. Enjoy warm with your favorite salad.

Nutritional Information (170g per serving):
Calories: 372| Fat: 27g| Sodium: 492mg| Carbs: 1g| Fiber: 0g| Sugars: 0g| Protein: 29g

Chapter 8: Vegetarian Recipes

Cauliflower Steak

Prep time: 20 minutes. | **Cook time:** 15 minutes. | **Serves:** 2

Ingredients:

- 1 head of cauliflower
- 2 tablespoons olive oil
- 1 teaspoon garlic powder
- 1 teaspoon smoked paprika
- ½ teaspoon salt
- ¼ teaspoon black pepper
- Optional toppings: chopped parsley, lemon wedges, grated Parmesan cheese

Directions:

1. At 375 °F, preheat your air fryer.
2. Remove all the exterior leaves from the cauliflower and trim the stem so that the cauliflower can lay flat.
3. Slice the cauliflower into 1-inch thick "steaks", starting from the center of the cauliflower and working outwards.
4. In a suitable bowl, mix olive oil, garlic powder, smoked paprika, black pepper and salt.
5. Brush both sides of the cauliflower steaks liberally with the seasoned oil.
6. Place the cauliflower steaks in the air fryer basket in one single layer, leaving some space between them for air circulation.
7. Cook in the air fry for 15 minutes, flip the steaks halfway through, until the cauliflower is tender and lightly browned.
8. Serve the cauliflower steaks hot with optional toppings.
9. Enjoy warm with your favorite dipping sauce.

Nutritional Information (100g per serving):
Calories: 140| Fat: 11g| Sodium: 610mg| Carbs: 10g| Fiber: 5g| Sugars: 4g| Protein: 4g

Broccoli Parmesan

Prep time: 15 minutes. | **Cook time:** 12 minutes. | **Serves:** 4

Ingredients:

- 1 head of broccoli, cut into florets
- 2 tablespoons olive oil
- ½ teaspoon garlic powder
- ½ teaspoon onion powder
- ¼ teaspoon red pepper flakes
- Salt and black pepper to taste
- ¼ cup grated Parmesan cheese

Directions:

1. At 375 °F, preheat your air fryer.
2. In a bowl, toss the broccoli florets with olive oil, garlic and onion powder, red pepper flakes (if using), black pepper and salt until evenly coated.
3. Place this seasoned broccoli in the air fryer basket in a single layer, with some space in between.
4. Cook in the air fry for 10 minutes, shaking the basket once cooked halfway through
5. Sprinkle grated Parmesan cheese over the broccoli and air fry for an additional 1-2 minutes until the cheese is melted and bubbly.
6. Serve the broccoli hot as a side dish or a snack.
7. Enjoy warm with your favorite salad.

Nutritional Information (113g per serving):
Calories: 180|Fat: 14g|Carbs: 10g|Fiber: 4g|Sugar: 2g| Protein: 6g

Stuffed Butternut Squash

Prep time: 20 minutes. | **Cook time:** 27 minutes. | **Serves:** 4

Ingredients:

- 1 butternut squash, halved and seeds removed
- 1 tablespoon olive oil
- ½ teaspoon garlic powder
- ½ teaspoon dried thyme
- ¼ teaspoon salt
- ¼ teaspoon black pepper
- ½ pound ground turkey or beef
- ½ onion, diced
- ½ cup chopped mushrooms
- ½ cup cooked quinoa
- ¼ cup chopped parsley
- ¼ cup grated Parmesan cheese

Directions:

1. At 375 °F, preheat your air fryer.
2. In a suitable bowl, mix olive oil, garlic powder, dried thyme, black pepper and salt.
3. Brush both sides of the butternut squash with the seasoned oil.
4. Place the butternut squash halves in the air fryer basket, cut side down, and air fry for 20 minutes, until the flesh is tender and lightly browned.
5. While the butternut squash is cooking, brown the ground turkey or beef in a skillet over medium heat until brown.
6. Add diced onion and chopped mushrooms to the skillet and air fry for 7 minutes, until the vegetables are softened.
7. Stir in cooked quinoa, chopped parsley, and grated Parmesan cheese.
8. Remove the butternut squash halves from the air fryer and fill each half with the turkey or beef mixture.
9. Place the stuffed butternut squash halves back in the air fryer basket, stuffing side up, and air fry for an additional 5-10 minutes, until the filling is heated through, and the cheese is melted.
10. Serve the stuffed butternut squash hot as a main dish or a side dish.

Nutritional Information (190g per serving):
Calories 351| Fat: 17.2g |Sodium: 475mg| Carbs: 25g| Fiber: 3.5g|Sugars: 2.4g |Protein: 28.8g

Fried Okra

Prep time: 15 minutes. | **Cook time:** 12 minutes. | **Serves:** 2

Ingredients:

- 1 pound fresh okra
- 1 tablespoon olive oil
- ½ teaspoon garlic powder
- ½ teaspoon onion powder
- ½ teaspoon paprika
- ¼ teaspoon salt
- ¼ teaspoon black pepper

Directions:

1. At 400 °F, preheat your air fryer.
2. Rinse the okra and pat dry with paper towels. Trim the ends off each pod.
3. In a suitable bowl, mix olive oil, garlic and onion powder, paprika, black pepper and salt.
4. Toss the okra in the seasoned oil, making sure each pod is coated evenly.
5. Place the seasoned okra in the air fryer basket in one single layer (without overlapping).
6. Air fry for 12 minutes, In order to achieve consistent cooking, shake the basket every 3 to 4 minutes.
7. Remove the cooked okra from the air fryer and transfer to a suitable plate lined with paper towels to absorb any excess oil.
8. Serve the okra hot as a side dish or a snack.
9. Note: You can modify the seasoning to your preferred flavor. If you like spicy food, you can add some cayenne pepper or chili flakes to the seasoning mix.
10. Enjoy with your favorite dipping sauce.

Nutritional Information (113g per serving):
Calories: 160| Fat: 7g| Sodium: 325mg| Carbs: 24g| Fiber: 11g| Sugars: 3g| Protein: 6g

Crusted Mushroom

Prep time: 15 minutes. | **Cook time:** 10 minutes. | **Serves:** 8

Ingredients:

- 8 large white mushrooms
- ½ cup almond flour
- ¼ cup grated parmesan cheese
- ½ teaspoon garlic powder
- ½ teaspoon onion powder
- ½ teaspoon dried thyme
- ½ teaspoon dried oregano
- ¼ teaspoon salt
- ¼ teaspoon black pepper
- 1 egg, beaten
- Cooking spray

Directions:

1. At 375 °F, preheat your air fryer.
2. Clean the mushrooms and remove the stems. Pat them dry with a paper towel.
3. In a suitable bowl, mix almond flour, grated parmesan cheese, garlic and onion powder, dried thyme, dried oregano, black pepper and salt.
4. Dip each mushroom cap in beaten egg, then coat it with the almond flour mixture. Make sure each mushroom is coated evenly.
5. Use a spritz of cooking spray to lightly grease your air fryer basket.
6. Place the coated mushroom caps in the air fryer basket in a single layer.
7. Air fry for 10 minutes, flip halfway through the cooking time to ensure even browning.
8. Remove the crusted mushrooms from the air fryer and transfer to a serving plate.
9. Enjoy it with your favorite dipping sauce.

Nutritional Information (110g per serving):
Calories: 165| Fat: 12g| Sodium: 290mg| Carbs: 8g| Fiber: 3g| Sugars: 2g| Protein: 9g

Mushroom Skewers

Prep time: 15 minutes. | **Cook time:** 10 minutes. | **Serves:** 6

Ingredients:

- 12 large button mushrooms
- 1 red onion, cut into wedges
- 1 red bell pepper, cut into chunks
- 1 yellow bell pepper, cut into chunks
- 2 tablespoons olive oil
- 2 tablespoons balsamic vinegar
- 1 teaspoon dried oregano
- ½ teaspoon garlic powder
- ½ teaspoon onion powder
- ¼ teaspoon salt
- ¼ teaspoon black pepper
- Skewers
- Cooking spray

Directions:

1. At 375 °F, preheat your air fryer.
2. Clean the mushrooms and remove the stems. Cut the larger mushrooms in half.
3. In a suitable bowl, mix well olive oil, balsamic vinegar, dried oregano, garlic and onion powder, black pepper and salt.
4. Add the mushrooms, red onion wedges, and bell pepper chunks to the bowl and toss until evenly coated.
5. Thread the vegetables onto skewers, alternating between mushrooms, onion wedges, and bell pepper chunks.
6. Use a spritz of cooking spray to lightly grease your air fryer basket.
7. Place the threaded vegetable skewers in the air fryer basket.
8. Air fry for 10 minutes, flip the skewers halfway through the cooking time to ensure even browning.
9. Serve hot as a side dish or an appetizer.
10. Enjoy with your favorite sauce.

Nutritional Information (100g per serving):
Calories 69.8| Fat 4.9 g| Sodium: 109.4 mg| Carbs: 6.2 g| Fiber 1.5 g| Sugars 3.1 g| Protein: 1.5 g

Eggplant Parmesan

Prep time: 15 minutes. | **Cook time:** 13 minutes. | **Serves:** 2

Ingredients:

- 1 large eggplant
- 1 cup almond flour
- ½ cup grated Parmesan cheese
- 2 eggs
- ½ teaspoon garlic powder
- ½ teaspoon dried basil
- ½ teaspoon dried oregano
- Black pepper and salt, to taste
- 1 cup low carb marinara sauce
- 1 cup shredded mozzarella cheese

Directions:

1. At 400 °F, preheat your air fryer.
2. Slice the eggplant into ¼ inch thick rounds.
3. In a shallow dish, mix well the almond flour, grated Parmesan cheese, garlic powder, dried basil, dried oregano, black pepper and salt.
4. In another shallow dish, beat the eggs.
5. Dip each eggplant slice into the beaten eggs, then coat in the almond flour mixture. Shake off any excess coating and place them onto a suitable plate.
6. Slices of eggplant should be sprayed on both sides with olive oil.
7. Place the eggplant slices in one single layer in the air fryer basket.
8. Air fry the eggplant slices for 10 minutes, flip halfway through, until they are crispy and golden brown.
9. Once all the eggplant slices are cooked, spread a thin layer of marinara sauce on top of each slice.
10. On top of the sauce, scatter some shredded mozzarella cheese.
11. Place the eggplant slices back into the air fryer and air fry for another 3 minutes.
12. If preferred, garnish with fresh basil leaves before serving.

Nutritional Information (120g per serving):
Calories: 423 | Fat: 28.6 g | Carbs: 20.8 g | Fiber: 11.1 g | Sugars: 9.7 g | Protein: 25.2 g

Ratatouille

Prep time: 15 minutes. | **Cook time:** 12 minutes. | **Serves:** 4

Ingredients:

- 1 medium zucchini
- 1 medium yellow squash
- 1 medium eggplant
- 1 red bell pepper
- ½ red onion
- 2 cloves garlic
- 2 tablespoons olive oil
- 1 teaspoon dried thyme
- ½ teaspoon dried basil
- ½ teaspoon dried oregano
- Black pepper and salt, to taste

Directions:

1. At 400 °F, preheat your air fryer.
2. Cut the zucchini, yellow squash, eggplant, and red bell pepper into ½-inch cubes. Cut the red onion into thin wedges. Mince the garlic.
3. In a suitable bowl, combine the cubed vegetables and minced garlic.
4. Olive oil should be poured over the vegetables, then mixed.
5. Add the dried thyme, basil, oregano, black pepper and salt to the bowl and toss to combine.
6. Spread the vegetables in one single layer in the air fryer basket.
7. Air fry the vegetables for 12 minutes, stirring halfway through, until they are tender and lightly browned.
8. Serve the ratatouille hot as a side dish or as a main course with a salad or grilled protein.
9. Enjoy your ratatouille!

Nutritional Information (100g per serving):
Calories 111 | Fat: 7g | Sodium: 4mg | Carbs: 11g | Fiber: 5g | Sugars: 6g | Protein: 3g

Tofu Satay

Prep time: 15 minutes. | **Cook time:** 10 minutes. | **Serves:** 4

Ingredients:

For the tofu:

- 1 block extra firm tofu, pressed and sliced into strips
- 1 tablespoon soy sauce
- 1 tablespoon olive oil
- ½ teaspoon garlic powder
- Black pepper and salt, to taste

For the satay sauce:

- ¼ cup natural peanut butter
- 2 tablespoons coconut aminos or soy sauce
- 1 tablespoon lime juice
- 1 teaspoon ChocZero maple syrup
- ¼ teaspoon ground ginger
- ¼ teaspoon garlic powder
- Water, as needed

Directions:

1. At 400 °F, preheat your air fryer.
2. In a bowl, mix well the soy sauce, garlic powder, olive oil, black pepper and salt. Add the tofu strips and toss to coat.
3. Place the tofu strips in one single layer in the air fryer basket.
4. Air fry the tofu strips for 10 minutes, flip halfway through, until they are crispy and golden brown.
5. While the tofu is cooking, make the satay sauce. In a suitable bowl, mix well the peanut butter, coconut aminos or soy sauce, lime juice, ChocZero maple syrup, ginger, and garlic powder. Add water as needed to thin the sauce to your desired consistency.
6. Serve the tofu strips hot with the satay sauce for dipping.
7. Enjoy your tofu satay!

Nutritional Information (100g per serving):
Calories: 227| Fat: 16g| Sodium: 440mg |Carbs: 6.9g|Fiber: 2.1g| Protein: 15.6g

Tofu Pineapple Skewer

Prep time: 10 minutes. | **Cook time:** 10 minutes. | **Serves:** 2

Ingredients:

- 1 block pressed (extra-firm) tofu, cut into 1-inch cubes
- ½ fresh pineapple, cut into 1-inch cubes
- 1 tablespoon olive oil
- 1 tablespoon soy sauce
- 1 tablespoon ChocZero maple syrup
- ½ teaspoon garlic powder
- Black pepper and salt, to taste
- Skewers

Directions:

1. At 400 °F, preheat your air fryer.
2. In a bowl, mix well the olive oil, soy sauce, ChocZero maple syrup, garlic powder, black pepper and salt.
3. Add the tofu and pineapple cubes to the bowl and toss to coat.
4. Thread the tofu and pineapple onto skewers, alternating between the two.
5. Place the skewers in one single layer in the air fryer basket.
6. Air fry the skewers for 10 minutes, flip halfway through, until the tofu and pineapple are lightly browned.
7. Serve the skewers hot as a snack, appetizer, or main course with a salad or low carb side dish.
8. Enjoy your tofu pineapple skewers!

Nutritional Information (150g per serving):
Calories: 326| Fat: 12g| Sodium: 529mg| Carbs: 44g| Fiber: 4g| Sugars: 35g| Protein: 14g

Crispy Broccoli Salad

Prep time: 10 minutes. | **Cook time:** 7 minutes. | **Serves:** 2

Ingredients:

For the broccoli:

- 1 head broccoli, chopped into florets
- 1 tablespoon olive oil
- Black pepper and salt, to taste

For the salad:

- 4 strips sugar-free bacon, cooked and crumbled
- ¼ cup diced red onion
- ¼ cup dried cranberries
- ¼ cup chopped pecans
- ½ cup mayonnaise
- 2 tablespoons apple cider vinegar
- 1 tablespoon low carb Swerve
- ½ teaspoon garlic powder
- Black pepper and salt, to taste

Directions:

1. At 375 °F, preheat your air fryer.
2. In a bowl, toss the broccoli florets with the olive oil, black pepper and salt.
3. Place this broccoli in one single layer in the air fryer basket.
4. Air fry the broccoli for 7 minutes, until it is tender and lightly browned.
5. In a suitable bowl, combine the cooked broccoli, crumbled bacon, diced red onion, dried cranberries, and chopped pecans.
6. In a suitable bowl, mix well the mayonnaise, apple cider vinegar, low carb Swerve, garlic powder, black pepper and salt.
7. Pour the prepared dressing over the broccoli salad and toss to coat.
8. Serve the broccoli salad chilled as a side dish or as a main course with grilled protein.
9. Enjoy your air fryer broccoli salad!

Nutritional Information (113g per serving):
Calories 288|Fat 21.6g|Sodium: 679mg|Carbs: 15g|Fiber 2.8g|Sugars 4.1g| Protein: 10g

Oyster Mushroom

Prep time: 10 minutes. | **Cook time:** 10 minutes. | **Serves:** 2

Ingredients:

- 8 ounces oyster mushrooms, cleaned and trimmed
- 2 tablespoons olive oil
- ½ teaspoon garlic powder
- Black pepper and salt, to taste

Directions:

1. At 375 °F, preheat your air fryer.
2. In a bowl, toss the oyster mushrooms with the olive oil, garlic powder, black pepper and salt.
3. Place the oyster mushrooms in one single layer in the air fryer basket.
4. Air fry the oyster mushrooms for 10 minutes, shaking the basket once cooked halfway through, until they are crispy and lightly browned.
5. Serve the oyster mushrooms hot as a snack or side dish with a low carb dipping sauce.
6. Enjoy your oyster mushrooms!

Nutritional Information (150g per serving):
Calories: 212| Fat: 22g| Sodium: 298mg| Carbs: 5g| Fiber: 2g| Sugars: 1g| Protein: 2g

Tofu Popcorn

Prep time: 10 minutes. | **Cook time:** 12 minutes. | **Serves:** 2

Ingredients:

- 1 block pressed extra firm tofu, cut into bite-sized cubes
- 1 tablespoon olive oil
- ¼ cup nutritional yeast
- ½ teaspoon garlic powder
- ½ teaspoon onion powder
- ½ teaspoon salt
- ¼ teaspoon black pepper

Directions:

1. At 400 °F, preheat your air fryer.

2. In a bowl, mix well the olive oil, nutritional yeast, garlic and onion powder, black pepper and salt.
3. Add the cut tofu cubes to the bowl and toss to coat.
4. Place the tofu cubes in one single layer in the air fryer basket.
5. Air fry the tofu cubes for 12 minutes, shaking the basket once cooked halfway through, until they are crispy and golden brown.
6. Serve the tofu popcorn hot as a low-carb snack or as a protein-rich topping for salads, bowls, or soups.
7. Enjoy your tofu popcorn!

Nutritional Information (100g per serving): Calories: 283| Fat: 16g| Sodium: 732mg| Carbs: 10g| Fiber: 4g| Sugars: 0g| Protein: 28g

Spicy Black Beans

Prep time: 10 minutes. | **Cook time:** 12 minutes. | **Serves:** 2

Ingredients:

- 1 can black beans, drained and rinsed
- 1 tablespoon olive oil
- ½ teaspoon cumin
- ½ teaspoon chili powder
- ½ teaspoon garlic powder
- Black pepper and salt, to taste

Directions:

1. At 400 °F, preheat your air fryer.
2. In a bowl, toss the black beans with the olive oil, cumin, chili powder, garlic powder, black pepper and salt.
3. Place the black beans in one single layer in the air fryer basket.
4. Air fry the black beans for 12 minutes, shaking the basket once cooked halfway through, until they are crispy and lightly browned.
5. Enjoy the black beans hot as a side dish or as a protein-rich topping for salads, bowls, or tacos.

Nutritional Information (70g per serving): Calories 84.25| Fat 3.75g|Sodium: 196.25mg|Carbs: 9.5g|Fiber 4.5g|Sugars 0.25g| Protein: 4.5g

Spaghetti Squash

Prep time: 15 minutes. | **Cook time:** 25 minutes. | **Serves:** 2

Ingredients:

- 1 spaghetti squash, halved and seeds removed
- 1 tablespoon olive oil
- Black pepper and salt, to taste

Directions:

1. At 375 °F, preheat your air fryer.
2. Brush the inside of the spaghetti squash halves with olive oil and season with black pepper and salt.
3. Place the spaghetti squash halves in the air fryer basket, cut side down.
4. Air fry the spaghetti squash for 25 minutes, until it is tender and the flesh easily pulls apart with a fork.
5. Allow the spaghetti squash cool for a few minutes, then use a fork to scrape the flesh into spaghetti-like strands.
6. Enjoy the spaghetti squash hot as a low carb pasta substitute, topped with your favorite low carb sauce and toppings.

Nutritional Information (150g per serving): Calories 70| Fat 7g|Sodium: 15mg|Carbs: 4g|Fiber 1g|Sugars 2g| Protein: 1g

Kale Potato Nuggets

Prep time: 10 minutes. | **Cook time:** 12 minutes. | **Serves:** 4

Ingredients:

- 1 large potato, peeled and grated
- 1 cup chopped kale
- ¼ cup almond flour
- 2 tablespoons coconut flour
- 1 egg, beaten
- ½ teaspoon garlic powder

- ½ teaspoon onion powder
- Black pepper and salt, to taste
- Olive oil or cooking spray

Directions:
1. At 375 °F, preheat your air fryer.
2. In a suitable bowl, mix the grated potato, chopped kale, almond flour, coconut flour, egg, garlic and onion powder, black pepper and salt.
3. Form the mixture into small nugget shapes, about 1-2 inches in size.
4. Spray the nuggets with cooking spray and place them in one single layer in the air fryer basket.
5. Air fry the nuggets for 12 minutes, flip halfway through, until they are crispy and lightly browned.
6. Enjoy the kale potato nuggets hot as a low carb snack or side dish, with your favorite dipping sauce.

Nutritional Information (100g per serving):
Calories 119| Fat 5 g| Sodium: 62 mg| Carbs: 14 g| Fiber 3 g| Sugars 1 g| Protein: 5 g

Buffalo Tofu

Prep time: 10 minutes. | **Cook time:** 12 minutes. | Serves: 2

Ingredients:
- 1 pressed block extra firm tofu, cut into 1-inch cubes
- ¼ cup hot sauce
- 1 tablespoon olive oil
- ½ teaspoon garlic powder
- Black pepper and salt, to taste
- Ranch or blue cheese dressing, for dipping

Directions:
1. At 400 °F, preheat your air fryer.
2. In a bowl, mix well the hot sauce, garlic powder, olive oil, black pepper and salt.
3. Add the diced tofu cubes to the bowl and toss to coat.
4. Place the tofu cubes in one single layer in the air fryer basket.
5. Air fry the tofu cubes for 12 minutes, shaking the basket once cooked halfway through, until they are crispy and lightly browned.
6. Enjoy the buffalo tofu hot, with ranch or blue cheese dressing for dipping if desired.

Nutritional Information (113g per serving):
Calories: 263| Fat: 18g| Sodium: 973mg| Carbs: 9g| Fiber: 2g| Sugars: 2g| Protein: 18g

Buffalo Cauliflower

Prep time: 10 minutes. | **Cook time:** 15 minutes. | Serves: 4

Ingredients:
- 1 head of cauliflower
- ½ cup almond flour
- ½ cup milk
- ½ cup breadcrumbs
- 1 teaspoon garlic powder
- 1 teaspoon paprika
- ½ teaspoon salt
- ¼ teaspoon black pepper
- ¼ cup buffalo sauce
- 2 tablespoons melted butter
- Ranch or blue cheese dressing, for serving

Directions:
1. At 400 °F, preheat your air fryer.
2. Cut the cauliflower into bite-sized florets.
3. In a shallow glass bowl, mix the flour, milk, garlic powder, paprika, black pepper and salt until smooth.
4. In another shallow bowl, place the breadcrumbs.
5. Dip each cauliflower floret in the flour mixture, then coat it with breadcrumbs.
6. Place the coated florets in the air fryer basket, making sure they are not overcrowded.
7. Cook the cauliflower for 15 minutes, shaking the basket occasionally, until they are golden brown and crispy.
8. In a suitable bowl, mix well the buffalo sauce and melted butter.

9. Once the cauliflower is cooked, remove it from the air fryer and place it in a suitable bowl. Pour the buffalo sauce mixture over the cauliflower and toss to coat evenly.
10. Serve hot with ranch or blue cheese dressing on the side.
11. Enjoy your delicious and healthy air fryer buffalo cauliflower!

Nutritional Information (113g per serving):
Calories: 270 | Fat: 14g | Sodium: 975mg | Carbs: 27g | Fiber: 7g | Sugar: 4g | Protein: 10g

Bang Bang Cauliflower

Prep time: 10 minutes. | **Cook time:** 12 minutes. | Serves: 4

Ingredients:

- 1 head of cauliflower, cut into florets
- ½ cup almond flour
- ½ teaspoon garlic powder
- ½ teaspoon paprika
- ½ teaspoon salt
- ¼ teaspoon black pepper
- 2 large eggs
- ¼ cup hot sauce
- ¼ cup mayonnaise
- 1 tablespoon ChocZero maple syrup
- 1 tablespoon rice vinegar
- 1 teaspoon Sriracha sauce (optional)

Directions:

1. At 400 °F, preheat your air fryer.
2. In a suitable bowl, mix well the hot sauce, mayonnaise, ChocZero maple syrup, rice vinegar, and Sriracha sauce (if using). Set aside.
3. In a separate bowl, mix well the almond flour, garlic powder, paprika, black pepper and salt.
4. In another bowl, beat the eggs.
5. Dip the cut cauliflower florets in the egg mixture, then coat it in the almond flour mixture.
6. Place the coated florets in the air fryer basket, making sure they are not overcrowded.
7. Cook the cauliflower for 12 minutes, shaking the basket occasionally, until they are golden brown and crispy.
8. Once the cauliflower florets are cooked, transfer them to a suitable bowl and pour the bang bang sauce over it. Toss to coat evenly.
9. Serve hot and enjoy your bang bang cauliflower!

Nutritional Information (160g per serving):
Calories: 423 | Fat: 32.1 g | Sodium: 762 mg | Carbs: 23.9 g | Fiber: 5.1 g | Sugars: 11.8 g | Protein: 13.9 g

Parmesan Brussel Sprouts

Prep time: 10 minutes. | **Cook time:** 15 minutes. | Serves: 2

Ingredients:

- 1 pound Brussels sprouts, trimmed and halved
- 2 tablespoons olive oil
- 1 teaspoon garlic powder
- 1 teaspoon onion powder
- 1 teaspoon paprika
- ½ teaspoon salt
- ¼ teaspoon black pepper
- Grated parmesan cheese

Directions:

1. At 400 °F, preheat your air fryer.
2. In a suitable bowl, toss the Brussels sprouts with olive oil until evenly coated.
3. In a suitable bowl, mix the garlic and onion powder, paprika, black pepper and salt.
4. Sprinkle the spice mixture over the Brussels sprouts and toss to coat evenly.
5. Place the Brussels sprouts in the air fryer basket, making sure they are not overcrowded.
6. Air fry the Brussels sprouts for 15 minutes, shaking the basket occasionally, until they are crispy and tender.
7. Once the Brussels sprouts are cooked, transfer them to a serving bowl and sprinkle with grated parmesan cheese.

8. Serve hot and enjoy your delicious Brussels sprouts!

Nutritional Information (200g per serving):
Calories: 393|Fat: 32.5 g| Sodium: 320mg |Carbs: 26 g|Fiber: 9 g|Sugar: 5 g | Protein: 10 g

Hush Puppies

Prep time: 10 minutes. | **Cook time:** 12 minutes. | **Serves:** 6

Ingredients:

- 1 cup almond flour
- ¼ cup coconut flour
- 1 teaspoon baking powder
- ½ teaspoon salt
- ½ teaspoon garlic powder
- ¼ teaspoon onion powder
- ¼ teaspoon cayenne pepper
- ½ cup unsweetened almond milk
- 1 egg, beaten
- ¼ cup finely chopped onion
- 1 tablespoon ChocZero maple syrup
- Cooking spray

Directions:

1. At 375 °F, preheat your air fryer.
2. In a suitable bowl, mix well the almond flour, coconut flour, baking powder, salt, garlic and onion powder, and cayenne pepper.
3. In a separate bowl, mix well the almond milk, egg, chopped onion, and ChocZero maple syrup.
4. Stir in the dry flour mixture and stir until just combined. Be careful not to overmix.
5. Use a tablespoon or cookie scoop to form the mixture into small balls.
6. Use a spritz of cooking spray to lightly grease your air fryer basket.
7. Place the hush puppies in one single layer in the air fryer basket.
8. Air fry for 12 minutes, flip the hush puppies over halfway through, until they are crispy and golden brown.
9. Serve the hush puppies hot as a side dish or snack.

Nutritional Information (100g per serving):
Calories: 181|Fat: 14g| Sodium: 386mg|Carbs: 11g|Fiber: 4g|Sugar: 4g| Protein: 6g

BBQ Lentil Meatballs

Prep time: 10 minutes. | **Cook time:** 12 minutes. | **Serves:** 6

Ingredients:

- 1 cup cooked lentils
- ½ cup breadcrumbs
- ½ onion, finely chopped
- 2 cloves garlic, minced
- 1 teaspoon smoked paprika
- 1 teaspoon dried oregano
- 1 teaspoon cumin
- ½ teaspoon salt
- ¼ teaspoon black pepper
- ¼ cup BBQ sauce

Directions:

1. At 400 °F, preheat your air fryer.
2. In a suitable bowl, mix the cooked lentils, breadcrumbs, onion, garlic, smoked paprika, oregano, cumin, salt, pepper, and BBQ sauce until well combined.
3. Use a cookie scoop or tablespoon to form the mixture into balls.
4. Place the meatballs in one single layer in the air fryer basket.
5. Air fry for 12 minutes, shaking the basket occasionally, until the meatballs are golden brown and crispy on the outside.
6. Serve the BBQ lentil meatballs hot as an appetizer or main dish, and enjoy!

Nutritional Information (120g per serving):
Calories: 217| Fat: 3.6g| Sodium: 609mg| Carbs: 36.7g| Fiber: 8.9g| Sugars: 8.6g| Protein: 11.2g

Crispy Soy Curls

Prep time: 15 minutes. | **Cook time:** 10 minutes. | Serves: 2

Ingredients:

- 1 cup soy curls
- 1 tablespoon soy sauce
- 1 tablespoon olive oil
- ½ teaspoon garlic powder
- ½ teaspoon onion powder
- ½ teaspoon smoked paprika
- ¼ teaspoon salt
- ¼ teaspoon black pepper

Directions:

1. At 375 °F, preheat your air fryer.
2. Place the soy curls in a suitable bowl, and cover them with hot water. Let them soak for 10-15 minutes, until they are tender and plump.
3. Drain the soy curls, and pat them dry with a paper towel.
4. In a separate bowl, mix well the soy sauce, olive oil, garlic and onion powder, smoked paprika, black pepper and salt.
5. Toss the soy curls into the bowl, and toss them with the seasoning mixture until they are evenly coated.
6. Place the soy curls in one single layer in the air fryer basket.
7. Air fry for 10 minutes, shaking the basket occasionally, until the soy curls are crispy and golden brown.
8. Serve the soy curls hot as a protein-rich snack or as a meat substitute in your favorite.

Nutritional Information (100g per serving):
Calories: 226|Fat: 11.7 g|Sodium: 226 mg |Carbs: 10.8 g|Fiber: 6.9 g|Sugar: 0.8 g| Protein: 22.6 g

Blooming Onion

Prep time: 10 minutes. | **Cook time:** 15 minutes. | Serves: 1

Ingredients:

- 1 large onion
- ½ cup almond flour
- ¼ cup grated parmesan cheese
- 1 teaspoon smoked paprika
- ½ teaspoon garlic powder
- ½ teaspoon salt
- ¼ teaspoon black pepper
- 2 eggs, beaten
- Cooking spray

Directions:

1. At 400 °F, preheat your air fryer.
2. Chop off the top of the onion, and peel off the outer layer.
3. Slice the onion into thin wedges, leaving about ½ inch of the onion intact at the bottom to hold the petals together.
4. In a shallow glass bowl, mix the almond flour, parmesan cheese, smoked paprika, garlic powder, black pepper and salt.
5. Dip each onion wedge into the beaten eggs, and then coat it with the almond flour mixture. Make sure the onion is well-coated.
6. Place this onion in the air fryer basket, and lightly spray it with cooking spray.
7. Air fry for 15 minutes, until the onion is tender and the coating is crispy and golden brown.
8. Carefully transfer the blooming onion to a suitable plate, and serve hot.

Nutritional Information (200g per serving):
Calories: 515| Fat: 36g| Sodium: 1244mg| Carbs: 29g| Fiber: 8g| Sugars: 7g| Protein: 23g

Chapter 9: Dessert

Walnut Brownie

Prep time: 10 minutes. | **Cook time:** 20 minutes.
Serves: 8

Ingredients:

- ½ cup almond flour
- ¼ cup coconut flour
- ½ cup unsweetened cocoa powder
- ½ teaspoon baking powder
- ¼ teaspoon salt
- ½ cup granulated Swerve
- ½ cup unsweetened applesauce
- 2 eggs
- 1 teaspoon vanilla extract
- ¼ cup chopped walnuts
- Cooking spray

Directions:

1. At 320°F, preheat your air fryer.
2. In a suitable bowl, mix the almond flour, coconut flour, cocoa powder, baking powder, salt, and granulated Swerve.
3. Add the applesauce, eggs, and vanilla extract to the bowl and whisk until smooth and well combined.
4. Fold in the chopped walnuts.
5. Grease a 6-inch cake pan or baking dish with cooking spray and pour the prepared brownie batter into it.
6. Place this cake pan or baking dish in the air fryer basket and air fryer it for 18-20 minutes.
7. To check if it's done from the center, insert a clean toothpick, and if it comes out clean, then your cake is done.
8. Let the brownie cool in the pan for 10 minutes before slicing and serving.
9. Serve these brownies with sugar-free chocolate syrup on top and enjoy.

Nutritional Information (90g per serving):
Calories: 120| Fat: 8g| Sodium: 110mg| Carbs: 10g| Fiber: 5g| Sugars: 2g| Protein: 6g

Carrot Cake with Cream Cheese Frosting

Prep time: 20 minutes. | **Cook time:** 35 minutes.
Serves: 8

Ingredients:

For the cake:

- 2 cups grated carrots
- ½ cup almond flour
- ¼ cup coconut flour
- ¼ cup granulated Swerve
- 1 teaspoon baking powder
- ½ teaspoon baking soda
- 1 teaspoon ground cinnamon
- ½ teaspoon ground ginger
- ¼ teaspoon ground nutmeg
- ¼ teaspoon salt
- 2 eggs
- ¼ cup unsweetened almond milk
- ¼ cup melted coconut oil
- 1 teaspoon vanilla extract
- Cooking Spray

For the frosting:

- 4 ounces cream cheese, softened
- 2 tablespoons unsalted butter softened
- ¼ cup powdered Swerve
- 1 teaspoon vanilla extract

Directions:

1. At 320°F, preheat your air fryer.
2. In a suitable plastic or glass bowl, mix the almond flour, coconut flour, granulated Swerve, baking powder, baking soda, cinnamon, ginger, nutmeg, and salt.
3. Add the grated carrots, eggs, almond milk, melted coconut oil, and vanilla extract to this bowl and stir until well combined.
4. Grease a 6-inch cake pan with cooking spray and pour the prepared batter into it.
5. Place this cake pan in the air fryer basket and air fry for 35 minutes. To check if it's done from the center, insert a clean

toothpick, and if it comes out clean, then your cake is done.
6. Let this air-fried cake cool in the pan for 10 minutes before placing it on a wire rack to cool.
7. To make this cake's frosting, beat the cream cheese and butter together in a suitable bowl until smooth.
8. Add the powdered Swerve and vanilla extract to the bowl and beat until well combined and fluffy.
9. Spread the frosting over the cooled cake.
10. Cut the cake into slices and serve.
11. Serve and enjoy your carrot cake.

Nutritional Information (100g per serving):
Calories: 149| Fat: 12g| Sodium: 176mg| Carbs: 8g| Fiber: 3g| Sugars: 2g| Protein: 4g

Zebra Cake

Prep time: 20 minutes. | **Cook time**: 35 minutes.
Serves: 8

Ingredients:

For the vanilla batter:

- 1 cup almond flour
- ¼ cup coconut flour
- ¼ cup granulated Swerve
- 1 teaspoon baking powder
- ¼ teaspoon salt
- 2 eggs
- ¼ cup unsweetened almond milk
- ¼ cup melted coconut oil
- 1 teaspoon vanilla extract

For the chocolate batter:

- 1 cup almond flour
- ¼ cup coconut flour
- ¼ cup granulated Swerve
- 1 teaspoon baking powder
- ¼ teaspoon salt
- 2 eggs
- ¼ cup unsweetened almond milk
- ¼ cup melted coconut oil
- ¼ cup unsweetened cocoa powder
- Cooking spray

Directions:

1. At 320°F, preheat your air fryer.
2. Grease a 6-inch cake pan with cooking spray.
3. To make the vanilla batter, mix the almond flour, coconut flour, granulated Swerve, baking powder, and salt in a suitable bowl.
4. Add the eggs, almond milk, melted coconut oil, and vanilla extract to the bowl and stir until well combined and smooth.
5. To make the chocolate batter, mix the almond flour, coconut flour, Swerve, baking powder, cocoa powder and salt in a suitable bowl.
6. Add the eggs, almond milk, and coconut oil to the bowl and stir until well combined and smooth.
7. Using a spoon or a cookie scoop, place 2 tablespoons of the vanilla batter into the center of the cake pan.
8. Then, place 2 tablespoons of the chocolate batter on top of the vanilla batter in the center of the pan. Continue alternating between the two batters, placing each spoonful directly on top of the previous spoonful until all the prepared batter is used up.
9. Tap the cake pan gently on a flat surface to level the prepared batter.
10. Place this cake pan in the air fryer basket and air fry for 35 minutes. To check if it's done from the center, insert a clean toothpick, and if it comes out clean, then your cake is done.
11. Let this cake cool in the pan for 10 minutes before placing it on a wire rack to cool completely.
12. Cut the cake into slices and serve.

Nutritional Information (100g per serving):
Calories 317| Fat 25.5g |Sodium: 286mg | Carbs: 12.2g| Fiber 6.1g | Sugars 0.3g | Protein: 9.8g

Cream Cheese Stuffed Lava Cake

Prep time: 15 minutes. | **Cook time:** 12 minutes.
Serves: 2

Ingredients:

- ¼ cup unsalted butter, melted
- 2 ounces sugar-free dark chocolate, chopped
- ¼ cup almond flour
- ¼ cup granulated Swerve
- 1 tablespoon unsweetened cocoa powder
- ¼ teaspoon baking powder
- ¼ teaspoon salt
- 1 large egg
- 1 teaspoon vanilla extract

Filling:

- 2 ounces cream cheese softened
- 1 tablespoon granulated Swerve
- Cooking spray

Directions:

1. At 350°F, preheat your air fryer.
2. Grease two 4-ounce ramekins with cooking spray.
3. In a microwave-safe bowl, melt the butter and chocolate together in the microwave, stirring every 30 seconds, until melted and smooth.
4. In a separate bowl, mix the almond flour, Swerve, cocoa powder, baking powder, and salt.
5. Add one large egg and vanilla extract to the dry ingredients and whisk until smooth.
6. Stir in the melted chocolate mixture to the bowl and whisk until well combined.
7. In another bowl, beat the cream cheese and Swerve together until smooth.
8. Fill each ramekin halfway with the chocolate batter.
9. Place a spoonful of the cream cheese mixture in the center of each ramekin.
10. Cover the cream cheese with the remaining chocolate batter.
11. Tap the ramekins gently on a flat surface to level the prepared batter.
12. Place these ramekins in the air fryer basket and air fry for 12 minutes, until the edges are set, but the centers are still slightly gooey.
13. Let the cakes cool for 5 minutes before serving.
14. Run any knife around the edges of the cooled ramekins and invert the cakes onto a suitable plate.
15. Enjoy with your favorite toppings.

Nutritional Information (100g per serving):
Calories 475| Fat 44g|Sodium: 320mg| Carbs: 19g| Fiber 4g| Sugars 1.01g| Protein: 9g

Chocolate Donut

Prep time: 20 minutes. | **Cook time:** 13 minutes.
Serves: 6

Ingredients:

For the donut:

- ½ cup almond flour
- ¼ cup cocoa powder
- ¼ cup granulated Swerve
- 1 teaspoon baking powder
- ¼ teaspoon salt
- ¼ cup unsweetened almond milk
- 2 tablespoons unsalted butter, melted
- 1 large egg
- ½ teaspoon vanilla extract
- Cooking spray

For the chocolate glaze:

- ¼ cup sugar-free chocolate chips
- 1 tablespoon coconut oil

Directions:

1. At 350°F, preheat your air fryer.
2. In a suitable bowl, mix the almond flour, cocoa powder, Swerve, baking powder, and salt until well combined.
3. In another bowl, mix the almond milk, melted butter, egg, and vanilla extract until smooth.
4. Stir in the dry flour mixture and whisk until a smooth batter forms.
5. Spray a silicone donut mold with cooking spray.
6. Spoon the prepared batter into the mold, filling each mold about 2/3 of the way full.

7. Place this mold in the air fryer basket and air fry for 12 minutes, until the donuts are set and spring back when lightly pressed.
8. Remove the air-fried donuts from the air fryer and let them cool in the mold for 5 minutes before removing them.
9. To make the donut's chocolate glaze, mix the chocolate chips with coconut oil in a microwave-safe bowl, and heat them to melt for 1-2 minutes, stirring every 30 seconds until melted.
10. Dip the tops of the air-fried donuts into the chocolate glaze and place them on a wire rack to set.
11. Enjoy the donuts once the glaze is set.

Nutritional Information (100g per serving):
Calories 121| Fat 11 g|Sodium: 184 mg| Carbs: 7 g| Fiber 3 g|Sugars 1 g| Protein: 4 g

Coffee Cake

Prep time: 10 minutes. | **Cook time:** 30 minutes.
Serves: 6

Ingredients:

For the cake:

- 1 ½ cups almond flour
- ½ cup granulated Swerve
- 2 teaspoons baking powder
- ½ teaspoon ground cinnamon
- ¼ teaspoon salt
- ¼ cup unsalted butter, melted
- ¼ cup unsweetened almond milk
- 2 large eggs
- ½ teaspoon vanilla extract

For the streusel topping:

- ¼ cup almond flour
- 2 tablespoons granulated Swerve
- 1 tablespoon unsalted butter, melted
- ½ teaspoon ground cinnamon
- Cooking spray or oil

Directions:

1. At 325°F, preheat your air fryer.
2. In a suitable bowl, mix the almond flour, Swerve, baking powder, cinnamon, and salt until well combined.
3. In another bowl, mix the melted butter, almond milk, eggs, and vanilla extract until smooth.
4. Stir in the dry flour mixture and whisk until a smooth batter forms.
5. In a suitable bowl, mix the almond flour, Swerve, melted butter, and cinnamon until well combined.
6. Grease an 8-inch baking pan with cooking spray or oil.
7. Spread half of the prepared cake batter into the pan.
8. Drizzle half of the streusel topping evenly over the prepared batter.
9. Pour the remaining batter over the streusel topping.
10. Sprinkle the remaining streusel topping over the top of the prepared batter.
11. Place the pan in the air fryer basket and cook for 30 minutes.
12. To check if it's done from the center, insert a clean toothpick, and if it comes out clean, then your cake is done.
13. Remove this pan from the air fryer and let this cake cool in the pan for about 10 minutes before slicing and serving.
14. Enjoy with your favorite beverage.

Nutritional Information (100g per serving):
Calories 397| Fat: 34.2g |Sodium: 293mg | Carbs: 11.1g | Fiber: 4.8g | Sugars: 0.3g | Protein: 12.3g

Shortbread Cookies

Prep time: 10 minutes. | **Cook time:** 10 minutes.
Serves: 8

Ingredients:

- 1 cup almond flour
- ¼ cup granulated Swerve
- ¼ teaspoon salt
- ¼ cup unsalted butter, melted
- ½ teaspoon vanilla extract

Directions:

1. At 300°F, preheat your air fryer.
2. In a suitable bowl, mix the almond flour, Swerve, and salt until well combined.

3. Add the melted butter and vanilla extract to the bowl and stir until a crumbly dough forms.
4. Use your hands to form the prepared dough into a ball.
5. Place the prepared dough ball on a piece of parchment sheet and use a rolling pin to roll the prepared dough out to about ¼ inch thickness.
6. With a cookie cutter or knife, cut the prepared dough into desired shapes.
7. Place the cookies on a piece of parchment paper and transfer them to the air fryer basket.
8. Air fry for 10 minutes until the edges are lightly golden.
9. Remove the cookies from the air fryer and let them cool on a wire rack.
10. Serve with your favorite beverage and enjoy.

Nutritional Information (54g per serving):
Calories: 116| Fat: 11g| Sodium: 74mg| Carbs: 3g| Fiber: 1g| Sugars: 0g| Protein: 3g

Butter Pecan Cake

Prep time: 20 minutes. | **Cook time:** 30 minutes.
Serves: 6

Ingredients:

For the cake:

- 1 ½ cups almond flour
- ½ cup granulated Swerve
- 2 teaspoons baking powder
- ½ teaspoon ground cinnamon
- ¼ teaspoon salt
- ½ cup unsalted butter, softened
- 3 large eggs
- ½ teaspoon vanilla extract
- ½ cup chopped pecans

For the topping:

- ½ cup chopped pecans
- 2 tablespoons granulated Swerve
- 2 tablespoons unsalted butter, melted
- ½ teaspoon ground cinnamon
- Cooking spray

Directions:

1. At 325°F, preheat your air fryer.
2. In a suitable bowl, mix the almond flour, Swerve, baking powder, cinnamon, and salt until well combined.
3. In another bowl, beat the softened butter with an electric mixer until creamy.
4. Add the eggs, one by one, and beat until well combined.
5. Pour in the vanilla extract and beat until well mixed.
6. Stir in the dry flour mixture and beat until a smooth batter forms.
7. Stir in the chopped pecans.
8. Grease an 8-inch baking pan with cooking spray.
9. Pour the prepared batter into the pan.
10. In a suitable bowl, mix the pecans, Swerve, melted butter, and cinnamon until well combined.
11. Sprinkle the pecan topping evenly over the top of the prepared batter.
12. Place the pan in the air fryer basket and cook for 30 minutes. To check if it's done from the center, insert a clean toothpick, and if it comes out clean, then your cake is done.
13. Remove this pan from the air fryer and let this cake cool in the pan for about 10 minutes before slicing and serving.
14. Serve and enjoy with your favorite warm beverage.

Nutritional Information (100g per serving):
Calories 403| Fat: 38.4g |Sodium: 190mg | Carbs: 8.5g | Fiber: 4.6g | Sugars: 0.9g | Protein: 9.2g

Churros

Prep time: 15 minutes. | **Cook time:** 10 minutes. | **Serves:** 6

Ingredients:

- 1 cup almond flour
- ¼ cup granulated Swerve
- ¼ teaspoon salt
- ¼ cup unsalted butter
- ½ cup water
- 1 teaspoon vanilla extract
- 1 egg
- ¼ cup cinnamon Swerve mixture

Directions:

1. At 350 °F, preheat your air fryer.
2. In a suitable-sized bowl, mix well the almond flour, Swerve, and salt.
3. In a suitable saucepan over medium heat, melt the butter with the water.
4. Remove this saucepan from the heat and stir in the vanilla extract and the dry ingredients until a dough forms.
5. Add the egg to the prepared dough and stir until fully combined.
6. Transfer the prepared dough to a piping bag fitted with a star tip.
7. Pipe 3-4 inch churros onto a sheet of parchment paper.
8. Place the churros into the air fryer basket and air fry for 7-10 minutes until golden brown.
9. Remove the churros from the air fryer and toss them in the cinnamon Swerve.
10. Serve warm and enjoy with a sugar-free chocolate dip!

Nutritional Information (70g per serving):
Calories: 320| Fat: 30g| Sodium: 230mg| Carbs: 12g| Fiber: 7g| Sugars: 0g| Protein: 7g

Low-Carbs Cupcakes

Prep time: 20 minutes. | **Cook time:** 15 minutes. | **Serves:** 6

Ingredients:

- 1 cup almond flour
- ¼ cup granulated Swerve
- ¼ cup unsalted butter, melted
- 1 teaspoon vanilla extract
- ¼ teaspoon salt
- ¼ teaspoon baking powder
- 2 eggs
- 2 tablespoons unsweetened almond milk

Directions:

1. At 320 °F, preheat your air fryer.
2. In a suitable-sized bowl, mix well the almond flour, Swerve, salt, and baking powder.
3. In a separate bowl, mix well the melted butter, vanilla extract, eggs, and almond milk.
4. Stir in the dry flour mixture and mix well until combined.
5. Spoon the prepared batter into silicone cupcake molds, filling each mold about 2/3 full.
6. Place the molds into the air fryer basket and air fry for 15 minutes.
7. To check the doneness, insert a toothpick to the middle of these cupcakes, if it comes out clean then they are done.
8. Remove the cupcakes from the air fryer and let them cool completely before serving.
9. Enjoy with your favorite frosting.

Nutritional Information (113g per serving):
Calories: 358|Fat: 33g| Sodium: 299mg| Carbs: 8g| Fiber: 3g| Sugars: 1g| Protein: 10g

Chocolate Chip Cookies

Prep time: 20 minutes. | **Cook time:** 10 minutes. | **Serves:** 6

Ingredients:

- 1 cup almond flour
- ¼ cup granulated Swerve
- ¼ teaspoon baking powder
- ¼ teaspoon salt
- ¼ cup unsalted butter, melted
- 1 egg
- 1 teaspoon vanilla extract
- ¼ cup sugar-free chocolate chips

Directions:

1. At 350 °F, preheat your air fryer.
2. In a suitable-sized bowl, mix well the almond flour, Swerve, baking powder, and salt.
3. In a separate bowl, mix well the melted butter, egg, and vanilla extract.
4. Stir in the dry flour mixture and mix well until combined.
5. Fold in the sugar-free chocolate chips.
6. Form the prepared dough into tablespoon-sized balls and place them onto a sheet of parchment paper.
7. Place the prepared dough balls into the air fryer basket and air fry for 10 minutes until golden brown.
8. Remove the cookies from the air fryer and let these cookies cool for a few minutes before serving.
9. Enjoy them with your favorite beverage.

Nutritional Information (32g per serving):
Calories: 268| Fat: 25g| Sodium: 208mg| Carbs: 10g| Fiber: 4g| Sugars: 2g| Protein: 6g

Blueberry Cobbler

Prep time: 10 minutes. | **Cook time:** 20 minutes. | **Serves:** 4

Ingredients:

- 1 ½ cups almond flour
- ¼ cup coconut flour
- ¼ cup granulated Swerve
- 1 teaspoon baking powder
- ½ teaspoon salt
- ½ cup unsalted butter, melted
- ¼ cup unsweetened almond milk
- 1 egg
- 1 teaspoon vanilla extract
- 2 cups fresh or frozen blueberries
- Cooking spray

Directions:

1. At 350 °F, preheat your air fryer.
2. In a suitable mixing bowl, mix well almond flour, coconut flour, Swerve, baking powder, and salt.
3. In a separate bowl, mix the melted butter, almond milk, egg, and vanilla extract.
4. Stir in the dry flour mixture and mix until a dough forms.
5. Fold in the blueberries.
6. Spray an air fryer-safe dish with cooking spray and transfer the prepared dough to the dish.
7. Place this dish in the air fryer basket and air fry for 20 minutes, until the cobbler is golden brown on top and the blueberries are bubbly.
8. Remove this cobbler from the air fryer and allow it to cool for a few minutes before serving.
9. Serve topped with sugar free whipped cream or low-carb ice cream if desired. Enjoy!

Nutritional Information (100g per serving):
Calories: 376| Fat: 34.3 g| Sodium: 356.5 mg| Carbs: 13.8 g| Fiber: 5.5 g| Sugars: 4.2 g| Protein: 7.4 g

Carrot Cupcakes

Prep time: 20 minutes. | **Cook time:** 18 minutes. | **Serves:** 6

Ingredients:
- ½ cup almond flour
- ¼ cup coconut flour
- ¼ cup granulated Swerve
- 1 teaspoon baking powder
- ½ teaspoon ground cinnamon
- ¼ teaspoon ground ginger
- ¼ teaspoon ground nutmeg
- Pinch of salt
- 2 eggs
- ¼ cup unsweetened almond milk
- ¼ cup coconut oil, melted
- 1 teaspoon vanilla extract
- 1 cup grated carrots
- Cooking spray

Directions:
1. At 320 °F, preheat your air fryer.
2. In a suitable mixing bowl, mix well almond flour, coconut flour, Swerve, baking powder, cinnamon, ginger, nutmeg, and salt.
3. In a separate bowl, mix eggs, almond milk, melted coconut oil, and vanilla extract.
4. Stir in the dry flour mixture and mix until well combined.
5. Fold in the grated carrots.
6. Grease a silicone muffin pan with some cooking spray and divide the prepared batter evenly among the cups.
7. Place this muffin pan in the air fryer basket and air fry for 15-18 minutes, until the cupcakes are golden brown.
8. Remove the muffin pan carefully from the air fryer and allow it to cool for a few minutes before serving.
9. Top with cream cheese frosting or whipped cream. Enjoy!

Nutritional Information (113g per serving):
Calories: 226| Fat: 20g| Sodium: 229mg| Carbs: 8g| Fiber: 4g| Sugars: 2g| Protein: 5g

Red velvet Cake

Prep time: 20 minutes. | **Cook time:** 25 minutes. | **Serves:** 6

Ingredients:

For the cake:
- 1 cup almond flour
- ¼ cup coconut flour
- ¼ cup granulated Swerve
- 1 teaspoon baking powder
- ½ teaspoon baking soda
- ¼ teaspoon salt
- 2 tablespoons unsweetened cocoa powder
- 2 eggs
- ¼ cup unsweetened almond milk
- ¼ cup coconut oil, melted
- 1 teaspoon vanilla extract
- 1 teaspoon apple cider vinegar
- Red food coloring (optional)

For the cream cheese frosting:
- 4 ounces cream cheese, softened
- ¼ cup unsalted butter, softened
- ¼ cup powdered Swerve
- 1 teaspoon vanilla extract

Directions:
1. At 320 °F, preheat your air fryer.
2. In a suitable mixing bowl, mix well almond flour, coconut flour, Swerve, baking powder, baking soda, salt, and cocoa powder.
3. In a separate bowl, mix eggs, almond milk, melted coconut oil, vanilla extract, and apple cider vinegar.
4. Stir in the dry flour mixture and mix until well combined.
5. If desired, add a few drops of red food coloring and mix until the prepared batter turns a deep red color.
6. Pour the prepared batter into a greased 6-inch cake pan.
7. Place this cake pan in the air fryer basket and air fry for 25 minutes, until the cake is cooked well.
8. Remove this cake pan from the air fryer and let cool completely.
9. Make the cream cheese frosting. In a suitable mixing bowl, beat together cream

cheese, butter, Swerve, and vanilla extract until smooth.
10. Once the cake has cooled, spread the cream cheese frosting evenly on top.
11. Garnish with fresh berries or whipped cream. Enjoy!

Nutritional Information (100g per serving):
Calories: 191| Fat: 17g| Sodium: 209mg| Carbs: 7g| Fiber: 3g| Sugars:- 1g| Protein: 5g

Cherry Pie

Prep time: 20 minutes. | **Cook time:** 30 minutes. | Serves: 6
Ingredients:
For the crust:
- 1 ½ cups almond flour
- ¼ cup coconut flour
- ¼ cup granulated Swerve
- ½ teaspoon salt
- ½ cup unsalted butter, melted
- 1 egg

For the filling:
- 3 cups fresh or frozen cherries, pitted
- ¼ cup granulated Swerve
- 2 tablespoons xanthan gum
- 1 tablespoon lemon juice
- 1 teaspoon vanilla extract
- Pinch of salt

Directions:
1. At 350 °F, preheat your air fryer.
2. In a suitable mixing bowl, mix well almond flour, coconut flour, Swerve, and salt.
3. Add melted butter and egg to the dry ingredients and mix until a dough forms.
4. Roll out the prepared dough on a floured surface and transfer to a greased 6-inch pie dish.
5. In a separate bowl, mix cherries, Swerve, xanthan gum, lemon juice, vanilla extract, and salt.
6. Fill the pie crust with the prepared cherry filling.
7. Bake the pie in the air fry for 30 minutes, until the crust is golden brown and the filling is bubbly.
8. Remove this pie from the air fryer and allow it to cool for a few minutes before serving.
9. Serve topped with sugar free whipped cream or low-carb ice cream if desired. Enjoy!

Nutritional Information (113g per serving):
Calories: 332|Fat: 28.3g|Carbs: 19g|Fiber: 5g|Sugars: 14g| Protein: 7g

Citrus Cake

Prep time: 20 minutes. | **Cook time:** 30 minutes. | Serves: 6
Ingredients:
For the cake:
- 1 ½ cups almond flour
- ¼ cup coconut flour
- ¼ cup granulated Swerve
- 1 teaspoon baking powder
- ¼ teaspoon salt
- 3 eggs
- ¼ cup unsweetened almond milk
- ¼ cup coconut oil, melted
- 2 tablespoons fresh lemon juice
- 2 tablespoons fresh orange juice
- 1 tablespoon lemon zest
- 1 tablespoon orange zest

For the glaze:
- ¼ cup powdered Swerve
- 2 tablespoons fresh lemon juice
- 1 tablespoon fresh orange juice

Directions:
1. At 320 °F, preheat your air fryer.
2. In a suitable mixing bowl, mix well almond flour, coconut flour, Swerve, baking powder, and salt.
3. In a separate bowl, mix eggs, almond milk, melted coconut oil, lemon juice, orange juice, lemon zest, and orange zest.
4. Stir in the dry flour mixture and mix until well combined.
5. Pour the prepared batter into a greased 6-inch cake pan.
6. Place this cake pan in the air fryer basket and air fry for 30 minutes, until the cake is cooked well.

7. While the cake is cooking, make the glaze. In a suitable mixing bowl, mix well powdered Swerve, lemon juice, and orange juice until smooth.
8. Drizzle the prepared glaze over the cake and let it set for a few minutes before serving.
9. Garnish with fresh berries or whipped cream. Enjoy!

Nutritional Information (100g per serving):
Calories: 249| Fat: 23g| Sodium: 113mg| Carbs: 8g| Fiber: 4g| Sugars: 2g| Protein: 7g

Chocolate Hazelnut Muffins

Prep time: 20 minutes. | **Cook time:** 18 minutes. | **Serves:** 6

Ingredients:
- 1 ½ cups almond flour
- ¼ cup coconut flour
- ¼ cup cocoa powder
- ¼ cup granulated Swerve
- 1 teaspoon baking powder
- ½ teaspoon baking soda
- ½ teaspoon salt
- 3 eggs
- ¼ cup unsweetened almond milk
- ¼ cup coconut oil, melted
- 1 teaspoon vanilla extract
- ½ cup sugar-free chocolate hazelnut
- Cooking spray

Directions:
1. At 325 °F, preheat your air fryer.
2. In a suitable mixing bowl, mix well almond flour, coconut flour, cocoa powder, Swerve, baking powder, baking soda, and salt.
3. In a separate bowl, mix eggs, almond milk, melted coconut oil, vanilla extract, and chocolate hazelnut spread.
4. Stir in the dry flour mixture and mix until well combined.
5. Grease a 6-cup muffin tin with cooking spray.
6. Fill each muffin cup approximately 3/4 full with the prepared batter.
7. Place this muffin tin in the air fryer basket and air fry for 15-18 minutes, until the muffins are cooked well and a toothpick inserted in the center comes out clean.
8. Once the muffins are cooked, let them cool for a few minutes.
9. Garnish with chopped hazelnuts or sugar-free chocolate chips. Enjoy!

Nutritional Information (113g per serving):
Calories: 211|Fat: 18g| Sodium: 249mg|Carbs: 9g|Fiber: 5g|Sugar: 1g| Protein: 8g

Cookie Cake

Prep time: 15 minutes. | **Cook time:** 25 minutes. | **Serves:** 4

Ingredients:
- ½ cup almond flour
- ¼ cup coconut flour
- ¼ cup Swerve
- ¼ teaspoon baking soda
- ¼ teaspoon salt
- ¼ cup unsalted butter, softened
- 1 egg
- 1 teaspoon vanilla extract
- ¼ cup sugar-free chocolate chips

Directions:
1. At 350 °F, preheat your air fryer.
2. In a suitable bowl, mix the almond flour, coconut flour, Swerve, baking soda, and salt.
3. Add the softened butter, egg, and vanilla extract. Mix well until a dough forms.
4. Fold in the sugar-free chocolate chips.
5. Form the prepared dough into a ball and place it in a greased 6-inch cake pan.
6. Place this cake pan in the air fryer and bake for 25 minutes until the cake is cooked through.
7. Remove the cooked cake from the air fryer.
8. Enjoy your delicious low-carb air fryer cookie cake!

Nutritional Information (100g per serving):
Calories: 175| Fat: 16 g| Sodium: 142 mg| Carbs: 7 g| Fiber: 3 g| Sugars: 1 g| Protein: 4 g

Pumpkin Pie Twists

Prep time: 20 minutes. | **Cook time:** 12 minutes. | **Serves:** 4

Ingredients:
- ½ cup almond flour
- ¼ cup coconut flour
- ¼ cup Swerve
- ½ teaspoon baking powder
- ¼ teaspoon salt
- ¼ cup unsalted butter, melted
- 1 egg
- ½ cup canned pumpkin puree
- 1 teaspoon pumpkin pie spice
- ¼ cup powdered Swerve
- 1 teaspoon cinnamon

Directions:
1. At 350 °F, preheat your air fryer.
2. In a suitable bowl, mix the almond flour, coconut flour, Swerve, baking powder, and salt.
3. Add the melted butter, egg, canned pumpkin puree, and pumpkin pie spice. Mix well until a dough forms.
4. Roll out the prepared dough into a rectangular shape on a flat surface.
5. In a suitable bowl, mix the powdered Swerve and cinnamon.
6. Sprinkle the cinnamon mixture evenly over the rolled out dough.
7. Cut the prepared dough into thin strips using a pizza cutter or knife.
8. Twist each strip of dough and place them in one single layer in your air fryer basket.
9. Air fry the pumpkin pie twists for 12 minutes until they are golden brown and cooked through.
10. Remove the twists from the air fryer once cooled.
11. Enjoy them with low-carb chocolate dip.

Nutritional Information (120g per serving):
Calories: 173| Fat: 15g| Sodium: 156mg| Carbs: 8g| Fiber: 3g| Sugars: 1g| Protein: 4g

Cinnamon Bread Twits

Prep time: 15 minutes. | **Cook time:** 12 minutes. | **Serves:** 4

Ingredients:
- ½ cup almond flour
- ¼ cup coconut flour
- ¼ cup Swerve
- ½ teaspoon baking powder
- ¼ teaspoon salt
- ¼ cup unsalted butter, melted
- 1 egg
- 1 teaspoon vanilla extract
- 1 teaspoon ground cinnamon
- 1 tablespoon powdered Swerve

Directions:
1. At 350 °F, preheat your air fryer.
2. In a suitable mixing bowl, combine the almond flour, coconut flour, Swerve, baking powder, and salt.
3. Add the melted butter, egg, and vanilla extract. Mix well until a dough forms.
4. Roll out the prepared dough into a rectangular shape on a flat surface.
5. In a suitable bowl, mix the ground cinnamon and powdered Swerve.
6. Sprinkle the cinnamon mixture evenly over the rolled out dough.
7. Cut the prepared dough into thin strips using a pizza cutter or knife.
8. Twist each strip of dough and place them in one single layer in your air fryer basket.
9. Air fry the cinnamon bread twists for 12 minutes until they are golden brown and cooked through.
10. Remove the twists from the air fryer before serving.
11. Serve and enjoy with low-carb chocolate dip.

Nutritional Information (120g per serving):
Calories: 198| Fat: 19g|Sodium: 151mg| Carbs: 6g| Fiber: 3g| Sugars: 1g| Protein: 4g

30 Days Meal-Plan

Day 1

Meal time	Recipe name	Pg No.	Calories
Breakfast	Pumpkin bread	16	182
Lunch	Chicken broccoli	35	326
	Eggplant parmesan	68	423
Snack	Cheese puffs	26	104
Dinner	Mongolian beef	56	324
Dessert	Cherry pie	84	332
Total calories			1691

Day 2

Meal time	Recipe name	Pg No.	Calories
Breakfast	English muffin	16	144
Lunch	Chicken teriyaki	36	362
Snack	Avocado fries	26	345
Dinner	Shrimp kung pao	50	221
	Bang Bang Cauliflower	73	423
Dessert	Citrus cake	84	249
Total calories			1744

Day 3

Meal time	Recipe name	Pg No.	Calories
Breakfast	Apple cobbler	17	336
Lunch	Stuffed chicken breast	36	525
Snack	Pickle fries	27	216
Dinner	Fried mahi-mahi	51	212
	Crusted Mushroom	67	165
Dessert	Chocolate hazelnut muffins	85	211
Total calories			1665

Day 4

Meal time	Recipe name	Pg No.	Calories
Breakfast	Banana churro oatmeal	17	185
Lunch	Dragon chicken	37	475
Snack	Kale chips	27	100
Dinner	Tofu Pineapple Skewer	69	326
	Pork skewers	61	390
Dessert	Cookie cake	85	175
Total calories			1651

Day 5

Meal time	Recipe name	Pg No.	Calories
Breakfast	Crunchy breakfast casserole	18	364
Lunch	Chicken meatloaf	37	275
	Stuffed Butternut Squash	66	351
Snack	Onion rings	27	276
Dinner	Maple glazed tuna steaks	51	350
Dessert	Pumpkin pie twists	86	173
Total calories			1789

Day 6

Meal time	Recipe name	Pg No.	Calories
Breakfast	Thai style omelet	18	315
Lunch	Spinach stuffed chicken	38	536
Snack	Plantains chips	28	184
Dinner	Crusted haddock	52	218
	Crispy Broccoli salad	70	288
Dessert	Cinnamon bread twits	86	198
Total calories			1739

Day 7

Meal time	Recipe name	Pg No.	Calories
Breakfast	Cheesy asparagus frittata	18	282
Lunch	Bacon wrapped chicken	39	682
Snack	Jalapeno poppers	28	332
Dinner	Crab stuffed mushrooms	53	103
	Teriyaki shrimp	46	158
Dessert	Walnut brownie	76	120
Total calories			1677

Day 8

Meal time	Recipe name	Pg No.	Calories
Breakfast	Scotch eggs	21	340
Lunch	Chicken breast asparagus rolls	39	396
Snack	Pepperoni chips	28	140
Dinner	Tuna patties	54	332
	Tofu Pineapple Skewer	69	326
Dessert	Carrot cake with cream cheese frosting	76	149
Total calories			1683

Day 9

Meal time	Recipe name	Pg No.	Calories
Breakfast	Omelet cups with bell pepper and onion	19	120
Lunch	Chicken drumsticks	39	271
Snack	Spicy peanuts	29	228
Dinner	Meatball subs	55	338
	Parmesan Brussel Sprouts	73	393
Dessert	Zebra cake	77	317
Total calories			1667

Day 10

Meal time	Recipe name	Pg No.	Calories
Breakfast	Egg and ham casserole	20	115
Lunch	Tandoori chicken	40	522
Snack	Chicken nuggets	29	278
Dinner	Garlicky buttery steak bites	55	387
	Mushroom Skewers	67	69
Dessert	Churros	81	320
Total calories			1691

Day 11

Meal time	Recipe name	Pg No.	Calories
Breakfast	Egg prosciutto	20	210
Lunch	Chicken mushroom skewers	41	197
Snack	Mozzarella sticks	30	238
Dinner	Steak tips with roasted potatoes	56	375
	Tofu Popcorn	70	283
Dessert	Cherry pie	84	332
Total calories			1635

Day 12

Meal time	Recipe name	Pg No.	Calories
Breakfast	Cauliflower hash brown	23	110
Lunch	Chicken satay	41	358
Snack	Carrot fries	30	64
Dinner	Bacon wrapped filet mignon	56	557
	Spicy Black Beans	71	84.5
Dessert	Coffee cake	79	397
Total calories			1570.5

Day 13

Meal time	Recipe name	Pg No.	Calories
Breakfast	Scotch eggs	21	340
Lunch	Chicken tenders	38	345
Snack	Bacon wrapped jalapeno peppers	31	91
Dinner	Mongolian beef	56	324
	Parmesan Brussel Sprouts	73	393
Dessert	Shortbread cookies	79	116
Total calories			1609

Day 14

Meal time	Recipe name	Pg No.	Calories
Breakfast	Broccoli frittata	21	300
Lunch	Crusted cod	47	338
Snack	Eggplant fries	32	256
Dinner	Pepperoni pizza	57	224
	Cauliflower Steak	65	140
Dessert	Butter pecan cake	80	403
Total calories			1661

Day 15

Meal time	Recipe name	Pg No.	Calories
Breakfast	Egg quiche	22	280
Lunch	Chicken cordon blue	42	404
Snack	Cassava fries	32	262
Dinner	Cheese stuffed kebabs	57	485
Dessert	Churros	81	320
Total calories			1751

Day 16

Meal time	Recipe name	Pg No.	Calories
Breakfast	Pumpkin bread	16	182
Lunch	Stuffed turkey rolls	43	445
Snack	Zucchini fritters	33	195
Dinner	Stuffed bell pepper	58	584
Dessert	Low-carbs cupcakes	81	358
Total calories			1764

Day 17

Meal time	Recipe name	Pg No.	Calories
Breakfast	Low carb flat-bread	23	210
Lunch	Duck breast fillet	45	516
Snack	Zucchini fritters	33	195
Dinner	Sweet sticky pork chops	58	312
	Tofu Pineapple Skewer	69	326
Dessert	Red velvet cake	83	191
Total calories			1750

Day 18

Meal time	Recipe name	Pg No.	Calories
Breakfast	Cauliflower hash brown	23	110
Lunch	Pesto chicken	44	440
Snack	Bacon wrapped zucchini fries	34	195
Dinner	Pork schnitzel	59	322
	Stuffed Butternut Squash	66	351
Dessert	Carrot cupcakes	83	226
Total calories			1644

Day 19

Meal time	Recipe name	Pg No.	Calories
Breakfast	English muffin	16	144
Lunch	Teriyaki shrimp	46	158
Snack	Cassava croquettes	34	351
Dinner	Beef Hamburgers	59	499
	Spaghetti Squash	71	70
Dessert	Blueberry cobbler	82	376
Total calories			1598

Day 20

Meal time	Recipe name	Pg No.	Calories
Breakfast	Kuku eggs	24	275
Lunch	Chicken casserole	44	452
Snack	Bacon wrapped avocado wedges	31	306
Dinner	Mushroom stuffed pork	60	398
Dessert	Chocolate chip cookies	82	268
Total calories			1699

Day 21

Meal time	Recipe name	Pg No.	Calories
Breakfast	Pumpkin bread	16	182
	Kuku eggs	24	275
Lunch	Herbed turkey breast	45	125
Snack	Bacon wrapped jalapeno peppers	31	91
Dinner	Roasted pork tenderloin	61	358
	Stuffed Butternut Squash	66	351
Dessert	Low-carbs cupcakes	81	358
Total calories			1740

Day 22

Meal time	Recipe name	Pg No.	Calories
Breakfast	English muffin	16	144
Lunch	Duck breast fillet	45	516
Snack	Eggplant fries	32	256
Dinner	Pork skewers	61	390
	Cauliflower Steak	65	140
Dessert	Churros	81	320
Total calories			1766

Day 23

Meal time	Recipe name	Pg No.	Calories
Breakfast	Apple cobbler	17	336
Lunch	Teriyaki shrimp	46	158
Snack	Cassava fries	32	262
Dinner	Pork mushroom skewer	62	374
	Ratatouille	68	111
Dessert	Butter pecan cake	80	403
Total calories			1644

Day 24

Meal time	Recipe name	Pg No.	Calories
Breakfast	Banana churro oatmeal	17	185
Lunch	Spinach stuffed salmon	46	540
Snack	Cauliflower croquettes	33	301
Dinner	Chimichurri lamb chop	62	483
	Spaghetti Squash	71	70
Dessert	Shortbread cookies	79	116
Total calories			1695

Day 25

Meal time	Recipe name	Pg No.	Calories
Breakfast	Omelet cups with bell pepper and onion	19	120
Lunch	Parmesan calamari	47	317
Snack	Zucchini fritters	33	195
Dinner	Beef fajita	63	443
	Kale Potato Nuggets	71	119
Dessert	Coffee cake	79	397
Total calories			1591

Day 26

Meal time	Recipe name	Pg No.	Calories
Breakfast	Thai style omelet	18	315
Lunch	Crusted cod	47	338
Snack	Bacon wrapped zucchini fries	34	195
Dinner	Lamb kebab	63	350
	Ratatouille	68	111
Dessert	Butter pecan cake	80	403

Day 27

Meal time	Recipe name	Pg No.	Calories
Breakfast	Cheesy asparagus frittata	18	282
Lunch	Crusted scallop	47	176
Snack	Cassava croquettes	34	351
Dinner	Beef meatloaf	64	350
	Mushroom Skewers	67	69
Dessert	Cream cheese stuffed lava cake	78	475
Total calories			1703

Day 28

Meal time	Recipe name	Pg No.	Calories
Breakfast	Egg, bean and mushroom burrito	19	150
Lunch	Fish schnitzel	48	332
Snack	Bacon wrapped avocado wedges	31	306
Dinner	Cauliflower steak	65	140
	Chimichurri lamb chop	62	483
Dessert	Zebra cake	77	317
Total calories			1728

Day 29

Meal time	Recipe name	Pg No.	Calories
Breakfast	Omelet cups with bell pepper and onion	19	120
Lunch	Shrimp fajita	48	243
Snack	Zucchini fries	25	303
Dinner	Bacon wrapped filet mignon	56	557
	Tofu Satay	69	227
Dessert	Carrot cake with cream cheese frosting	76	149
Total calories			1599

Day 30

Meal time	Recipe name	Pg No.	Calories
Breakfast	Egg and ham casserole	20	115
Lunch	Chicken Kiev	35	554
	Stuffed butternut squash	66	351
Snack	Chicken samosa	25	99
Dinner	Pork skewers	61	390
Dessert	Walnut brownie	76	120
Total calories			1629

30 Days Shopping

Fruits

2 lbs. apples
2 lbs. bananas
3 lbs. avocado
10 lemons
10 limes
3 pineapples
5 pints of berries (blueberries, strawberries, raspberries, etc.)

Vegetables:

12 lbs. of potatoes
6 lbs. of carrots
6 lbs. of onions
6 heads of garlic
6 bags of spinach
6 bunches of kale
10 bunches of broccoli
12 cauliflower heads
3 lbs. of green beans
3 lbs. of asparagus
3 lbs. of brussels sprouts
2 lb. snap peas pod
2 lbs. bell peppers
8 lbs. zucchini
4 lbs. eggplant
2 spaghetti squash
2 butternut squash
16 ounces oyster mushrooms
44 button mushrooms
24 small button mushrooms
40 large mushrooms
1 cup baby portobello mushrooms
2 bunches fresh cilantro
2 bunches fresh parsley
3 bunches fresh basil
3 cups shredded lettuce
3 cups jalapenos
3 bunches spring onion
6 cups celery

Dairy:

3 gallons of milk
6 dozen eggs
1/2 cup coconut milk
3 blocks of cheddar cheese
15 oz. parmesan cheese
1 lb. mozzarella cheese
2 cups cream cheese
3 cups heavy cream
8 slices provolone cheese
2 containers of sour cream
6 sticks of butter

Proteins:

12 lbs. of chicken breasts
2 whole chickens
6 pounds turkey breast
24 oz. duck breast fillets
6 lbs. of ground beef
2 lbs. ground lamb
4 lbs. ground chicken
24 oz. tilapia fish
2 lbs. ground turkey
6 lbs. chicken thighs
6 lbs. beef steak
1 lb. beef filet mignon
8 lbs. of pork chops
4 lbs. of bacon
2 lbs. of deli meat (ham or turkey)
8 lbs. pork tenderloin
2 lbs. tofu
16 ounces lump crab meat
8 lbs. salmon fillets
6 lbs. shrimp
4 lbs. scallops
24 prosciutto slices
2 lbs. haddock
2 lbs. cod
4 lbs. tuna
1 lb. pepperoni slices

Fats:

4 cups olive oil
1/2 cup sesame oil
1/2 cup sunflower oil

Canned And Dry Goods:

4 cans of black beans
2 cans sun-dried tomatoes
4 cans of chickpeas
4 cans of diced tomatoes
4 cans of tomato sauce
2 jars of pasta sauce
2 packages of corn tortillas
2 jars of peanut butter
1 jar pizza sauce

Flours

5 lbs. almond flour
5 lbs. coconut flour
2 lbs. oat flour
4 lbs. breadcrumbs
1 lb. quinoa
12 hoagie rolls

Sweeteners:

2 (12 oz.) packs granulated swerve
1 (12 oz.) pack brown swerve
2 (12 oz.) packs powdered swerve
1 bottle choc zero maple syrup

Nuts And Seeds

2 cup almonds
½ cup sesame seeds
1 cup pecans
1 cup dried cranberries
1 cup raisins
½ cup walnuts

Miscellaneous

¼ cup apple cider vinegar
¼ cup apple sauce (unsweetened)
¼ cup balsamic vinegar
¼ cup garam masala
¼ cup ground coriander
¼ cup lemon juice
¼ cup rice vinegar
¼ cup sriracha sauce
¼ cup turmeric powder
¼ cup Worcestershire sauce
½ cup basil pesto
½ cup red wine vinegar
1 cup bbq sauce
1 cup black pepper
1 cup salt
1 cup buffalo sauce
1 cup cumin
1 cup dried thyme
1 cup garlic powder
1 cup ginger powder
1 cup ground cumin
1 cup hot sauce
1 cup onion powder
1 cup paprika
1 cup smoked paprika
1 cup xanthan gum
1/4 cup Cajun seasoning
1/4 cup chili powder
1/4 cup dried basil
1/4 cup dried oregano
1/4 cup dried rosemary
1/4 cup dried sage
1/4 cup Italian seasoning
1/4 cup lime juice
2 cups mayonnaise
2 cups soy sauce
2 jars low-carb marinara sauce
24 wonton wrappers

Measurement Conversion Table

Weight conversion tables

Pounds (lbs)	Ounces (oz)	Grams (g)
1	16	453.6
2	32	907.2
3	48	1360.8
4	64	1814.4
5	80	2268.0

Kilograms (kg)	Pounds (lbs)	Ounces (oz)	Grams (g)
0.5	1.1	17.6	500
1	2.2	35.3	1000
1.5	3.3	52.9	1500
2	4.4	70.5	2000
2.5	5.5	88.2	2500
3	6.6	105.8	3000

Ounces (oz)	Grams (g)	Tablespoons (tbsp)	Teaspoons (tsp)
0.5	14.2	1	3
1	28.4	2	6
1.5	42.5	3	9
2	56.7	4	12
2.5	70.9	5	15
3	85.0	6	18
3.5	99.2	7	21
4	113.4	8	24
4.5	127.6	9	27
5	141.7	10	30

Liquid Conversion Table

Measurement	Metric	US Customary	Imperial
Teaspoon (tsp)	5 ml	1/6 fl oz	1/6 fl oz
Tablespoon (tbsp)	15 ml	1/2 fl oz	1/2 fl oz
Fluid Ounce (fl oz)	30 ml	1 fl oz	1.04 fl oz
Cup (c)	240 ml	8 fl oz	9.61 fl oz
Pint (pt)	473 ml	16 fl oz	19.22 fl oz
Quart (qt)	946 ml	32 fl oz	38.43 fl oz
Liter (l)	1000 ml	33.814 fl oz	35.195 fl oz
Gallon (gal)	3.785 l	128 fl oz	153.72 fl oz

Conclusion

Now that you have gone through all the delicious, easy-to-try air fryer recipes from this cookbook- have you picked your favorite ones yet? Well, you can always mix and match the different recipe ideas from this cookbook to create a menu of your own or simply stick to the 30 days meal plan. I added this meal plan just to help you get started with your diabetic-friendly diet and to help you maintain your daily calorie intake. You can always add a low-carb smoothie of your choice between breakfast and lunch times to keep yourselves nourished. Dealing with diabetes while eating healthy is indeed challenging, and I wanted to make sure that you get all the support that you need to make the necessary changes in your daily diet.

Perhaps the whole idea of this Diabetic Air fryer recipes cookbook revolves around one single goal- that is to provide healthy and nourishing meal options without letting you miss any of the good flavors. From breakfast to snacks to meat, seafood, poultry, vegetarian, and dessert recipes, there is something for everyone in this cookbook. It's about time to put on aprons, get all the ingredients, and create some flavorsome magic with your air fryers!

DOWNLOAD YOUR GIFTS NOW!

The bonuses are 100% FREE

Unlock your exclusive bonuses NOW

by scanning the QR code!

Or go to bookisho.com/DAF-amazon

Recipes in Alphabetical Order

Apple Cobbler	17
Avocado Fries	26
Bacon Wrapped Avocado Wedge	31
Bacon Wrapped Chicken	39
Bacon Wrapped Filet Mignon	56
Bacon Wrapped Jalapeno Peppers	31
Bacon Wrapped Pork Tenderloin	61
Bacon Wrapped Scallop	50
Bacon Wrapped Shrimp	49
Bacon Wrapped Zucchini Fries	34
Banana Churro Oatmeal	17
Bang Bang Cauliflower	73
BBQ Lentil Meatballs	74
Beef Fajita	63
Beef Hamburgers	59
Beef Meatloaf	64
Blackened Salmon	54
Blooming Onion	75
Blueberry Cobbler	82
Broccoli Frittata	21
Broccoli Parmesan	65
Buffalo Cauliflower	72
Buffalo Tofu	72
Butter Pecan Cake	80
Cajun Pork Chops	64
Carrot Cake with Cream Cheese Frosting	76
Carrot Cupcakes	83
Carrot Fries	30
Cassava Croquettes	34
Cassava Fries	32
Cauliflower Croquettes	33
Cauliflower Hash Brown	23
Cauliflower Steak	65
Cheese Puffs	26
Cheese Stuffed Kebabs	57
Cheesy Asparagus Frittata	18
Cherry Pie	84
Chicken Breast Asparagus Rolls	39
Chicken Broccoli	35
Chicken Casserole	44
Chicken Cordon Blue	42
Chicken Drumsticks	39
Chicken Fajita	42
Chicken Kiev	35
Chicken Meatloaf	37
Chicken Mushroom Skewers	41
Chicken Nuggets	29
Chicken Parmesan	44
Chicken Samosa	25
Chicken Satay	41
Chicken Tenders	38
Chicken Teriyaki	36
Chimichurri Lamb Chop	62
Chocolate Chip Cookies	82
Chocolate Donut	78
Chocolate Hazelnut Muffins	85
Churros	81
Cinnamon Bread Twits	86
Citrus Cake	84
Coffee Cake	79
Cookie Cake	85
Crab Rangoon	53
Crab Stuffed Mushrooms	53
Cream Cheese Stuffed Lava Cake	78
Crispy Broccoli Salad	70
Crispy Oysters	52
Crispy Soy Curls	75
Crunchy Breakfast Casserole	18
Crusted Cod	47
Crusted Haddock	52
Crusted Mushroom	67
Crusted Scallops	47
Dragon Chicken	37
Duck Breast Fillet	45
Egg and Ham Casserole	20
Egg Bites	20
Egg Prosciutto	20
Egg Quiche	22
Egg Zucchini Frittata	24
Egg, Bean and Mushroom Burrito	19
Eggplant Fries	32
Eggplant Parmesan	68
English Muffin	16

Fish Schnitzel	48
Fish Sticks	50
Fish Tacos	49
Fried Mahi-Mahi	51
Fried Okra	66
Garlicky Buttery Steak Bites	55
Herbed Turkey Breast	45
Hush Puppies	74
Jalapeno Poppers	28
Kale Chips	27
Kale Potato Nuggets	71
Kuku Eggs	24
Lamb Kebab	63
Low Carb Flat-Bread	23
Low-Carb Granola	22
Low-Carbs Cupcakes	81
Maple Glazed Tuna Steaks	51
Meatball Subs	55
Mongolian Beef	56
Mozzarella Sticks	30
Mushroom Skewers	67
Mushroom Stuffed Pork	60
Omelet Cups with Bell Pepper and Onion	19
Onion Rings	27
Oyster Mushroom	70
Parmesan Brussel Sprouts	73
Parmesan Calamari	47
Pepperoni Chips	28
Pepperoni Pizza	57
Pesto Chicken	44
Pickle Fries	27
Plantains Chips	28
Pork Mushroom Skewer	62
Pork Schnitzel	59
Pork Skewers	61
Pumpkin Bread	16
Pumpkin Pie Twists	86
Ratatouille	68
Red velvet Cake	83
Roasted Pork Tenderloin	61
Scotch Eggs	21
Shortbread Cookies	79
Shrimp Fajita	48
Shrimp Kung Pao	50
Spaghetti Squash	71
Spicy Black Beans	71
Spicy Peanuts	29
Spinach Stuffed Chicken	38
Spinach Stuffed Salmon	46
Steak Tips with Roasted Potatoes	56
Stuffed Bell Pepper	58
Stuffed Butternut Squash	66
Stuffed Chicken Breast	36
Stuffed Turkey Rolls	43
Stuffed Whole Chicken	43
Sweet Sticky Pork Chops	58
Tandoori Chicken	40
Teriyaki Shrimp	46
Thai Style Omelet	18
Tofu Pineapple Skewer	69
Tofu Popcorn	70
Tofu Satay	69
Tuna Patties	54
Walnut Brownie	76
Zebra Cake	77
Zucchini Fries	25

SP

Printed in Great Britain
by Amazon